BUILD A DREAM
ARCHITECTURE + DESIGN FOR KIDS

Editor-in-chief: Y&Y (Yang Liu & Jianing Yuan)
Editor: Heng Zhang
Proofreader: Heng Zhang
Art Director: Yannick (Jianing Yuan)
Design Director: Yang Liu
Printing Specialist: Yang Liu
Design and Layout: Heng Zhang, Yang Liu

Publisher: DESIGNERBOOKS
Unit D, 16/F, Cheuk Nang 21st Century Plaza, 250 Hennessy Road,
Wanchai, Hong Kong
Tel: +852-2575-5186
Fax: +852-2891-1996
E-mail: edit@designerbooks.com.cn

Distributor: DESIGNERBOOKS
Rm. 504-505, Bld. C, International Negotiate Garden,
NO. 3, Jinguanbei'er Str., Shunyi Dist., Beijing, China
Tel: 0086-10-6400-3080 (Beijing)
       0086-21-5596-7639 (Shanghai)
       0086-755-8825-0425 (Shenzhen)
       0086-20-8756-5010 (Guangzhou)
Fax: 0086-10-64018430-822
E-mail: import01@designerbooks.com.cn
http://www.designerbooks.com.cn

Printed in China

All rights reserved. No part of this publication may be reproduced in any form or by any means, graphic, electronic or mechanical, including photocopying and recording by an information storage and retrieval system without permission in writing from the publisher.

ISBN: 978-988-77706-6-4
Copyright © 2018 by DESIGNERBOOKS

BUILD A DREAM

ARCHITECTURE + DESIGN FOR KIDS

A day care is one of the first spaces a child discovers outside the family unit. It must be able to provide an atmosphere which both reassures and helps children grow, while protecting and exposing them to the outside world.

Developing the project we encountered urban constraints: The site is located at the center of the Fréquel Fontarabie district, an ecological area in the heart of Paris, and at the intersection of a public thoroughfare and a public square. Therefore, the new building was going to influence the identity of the district's central space, its garden and the plot.

In order to comply with the Local Urban Plan (PLU) we chose to distribute the volume of the childcare area onto two floors. We located the director's apartment on a 3rd and 4th floor so as to respect the required height of twelve meters over the square, with a north/south orientation.

Because the building is long, a "patio" was necessary in order to bring natural light into the service rooms. This open space also has a role in temperature regulation, especially in the summer.

For acoustic and thermal reasons, the structure of the building was made in concrete, lined with insulation and metal cladding. This wall of perforated steel creates different lighting effects and it works as a filter that provides privacy. The garden and terraces are widely accessible through large openings.

The garden at the end of the plot is composed of a central maple tree and shrubs that grow on sloping land, leading to an exit onto a public passage.

Day Care Rue Des Orteaux

Architects : Avenier Cornejo
Country : France
Photographer : David Foessel, Julien Lanoo
Site surface : 865m²
Built surface : 1037.5m²
Project Team : LGX [BET TCE], CAP TERRE [HQE]
Client : SLA20 – Section local de l' architecture de la Ville de Paris

Day Care Rue Des Orteaux

Architects : Avenier Cornejo
Country : France

Day Care Rue Des Orteaux

Architects : Avenier Cornejo
Country : France

Day Care Rue Des Orteaux

Architects : Avenier Cornejo
Country : France

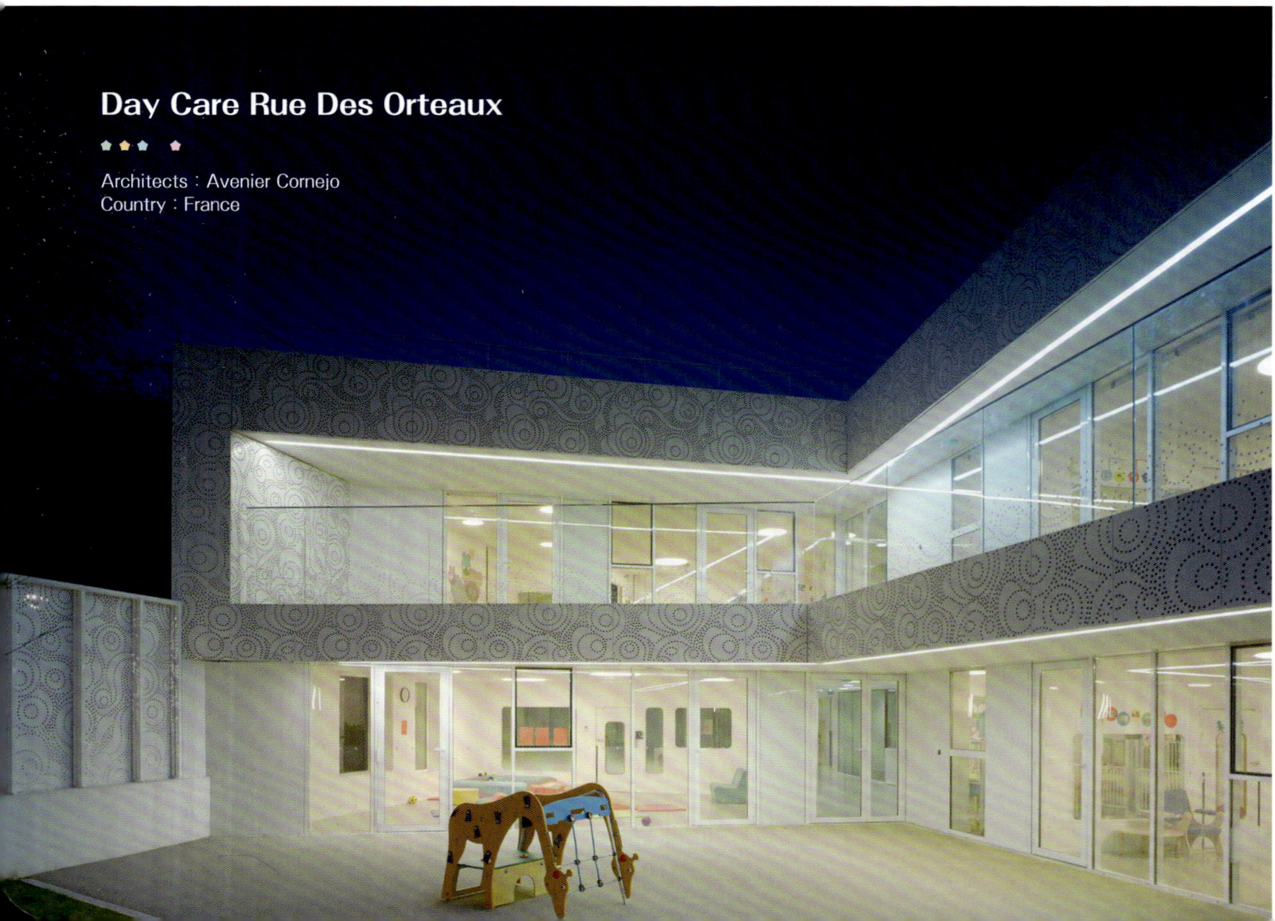

11

Day Care Rue Des Orteaux

Architects : Avenier Cornejo
Country : France

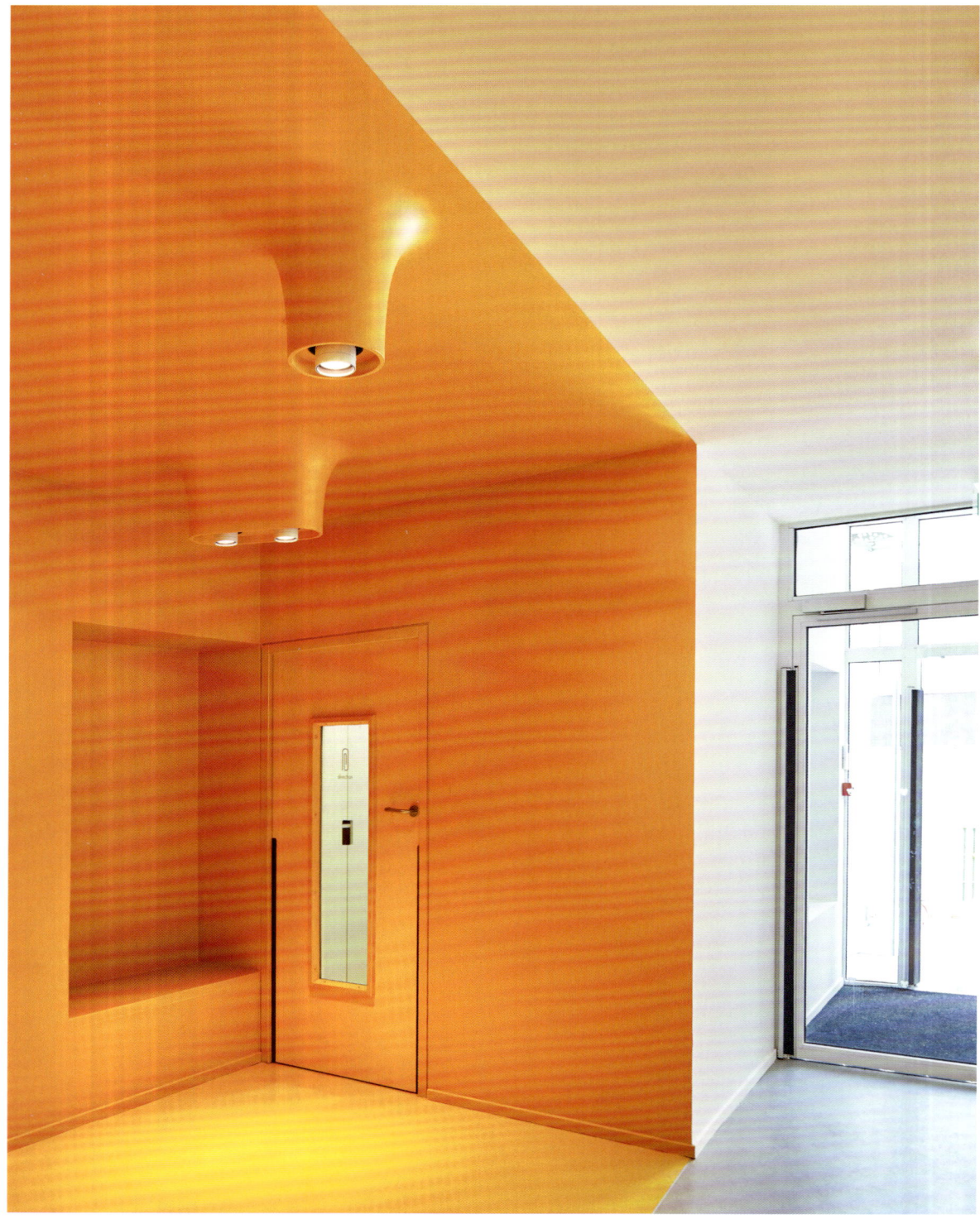

Day Care Rue Des Orteaux

Architects : Avenier Cornejo
Country : France

Educational Training Centre for Professional and Working Skills

The Educational Training Centre for Professional and Working Skills is one of the state of the art educational institutions in Serbia and the region. It was founded by the Government of the Autonomous Province of Vojvodina and is aimed at providing professional education and training for unemployed and employed persons.

Our objectives are to prevent long-term unemployment; provide assistance in attainment of new knowledge and skills aimed at increasing employment chances; provide support in entrepreneurial development and creation of preconditions for starting business; and quality investment in training and education of the unemployed. We promote the personal and professional development of persons who attend our courses and offer them high-quality education through practice-oriented courses.

Architects : Nikola Martinovic
Country : Serbia
Design Agency : NMARTIN architectural studio
Photographer : Nikola Martinovic
Client : Educational Training Centre - Novi Sad

Educational Training Centre for Professional and Working Skills

Architects : Nikola Martinovic
Country : Serbia

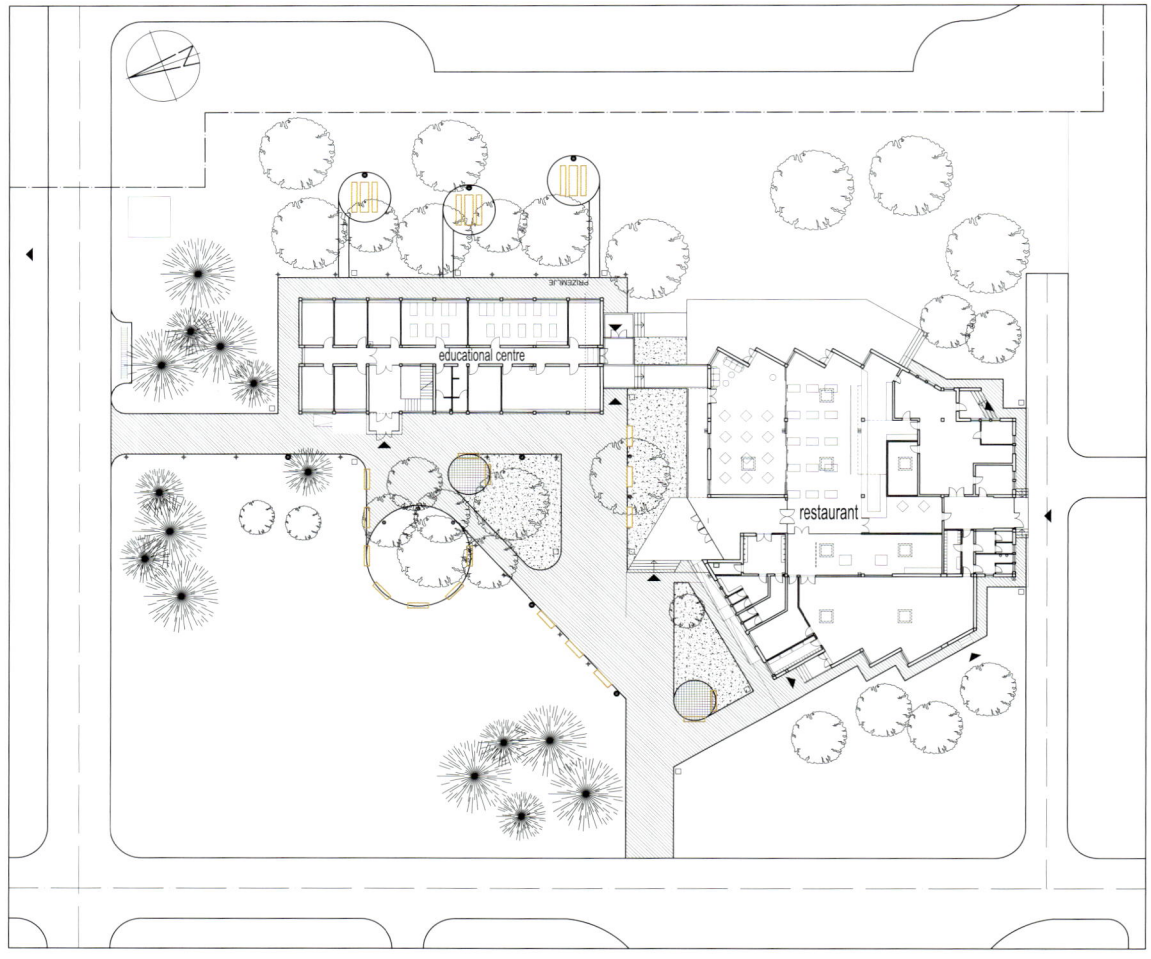

Educational Training Centre for Professional and Working Skills

Architects : Nikola Martinovic
Country : Serbia

Educational Training Centre for Professional and Working Skills

Architects : Nikola Martinovic
Country : Serbia

Educational Training Centre for Professional and Working Skills

Architects : Nikola Martinovic
Country : Serbia

GROUND FLOOR

MAIN ENTRANCE

FIRST FLOOR

SECOND FLOOR

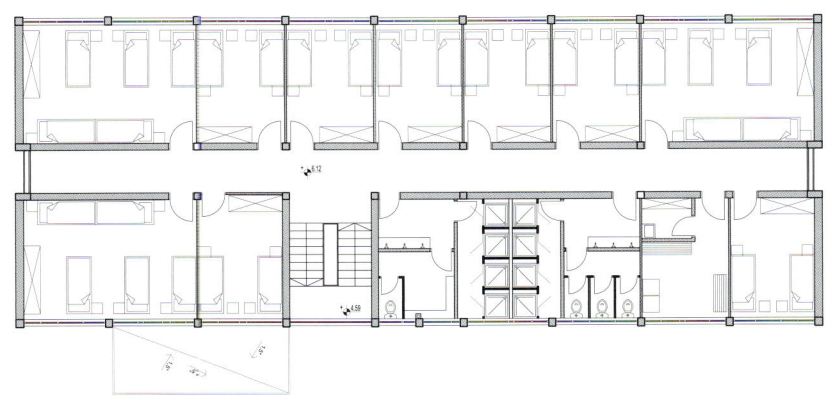

Educational Training Centre for Professional and Working Skills

Architects : Nikola Martinovic
Country : Serbia

Educational Training Centre for Professional and Working Skills

Architects : Nikola Martinovic
Country : Serbia

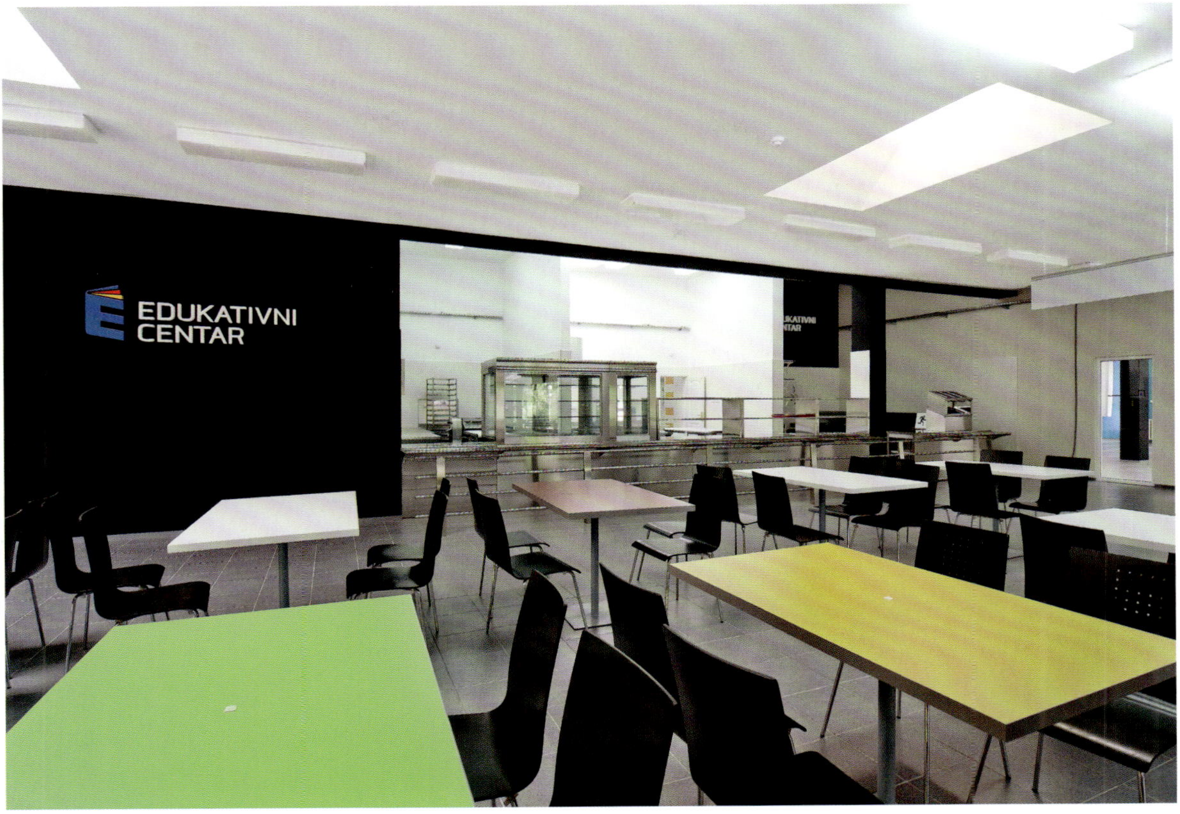
EDUKATIVNI
CENTAR

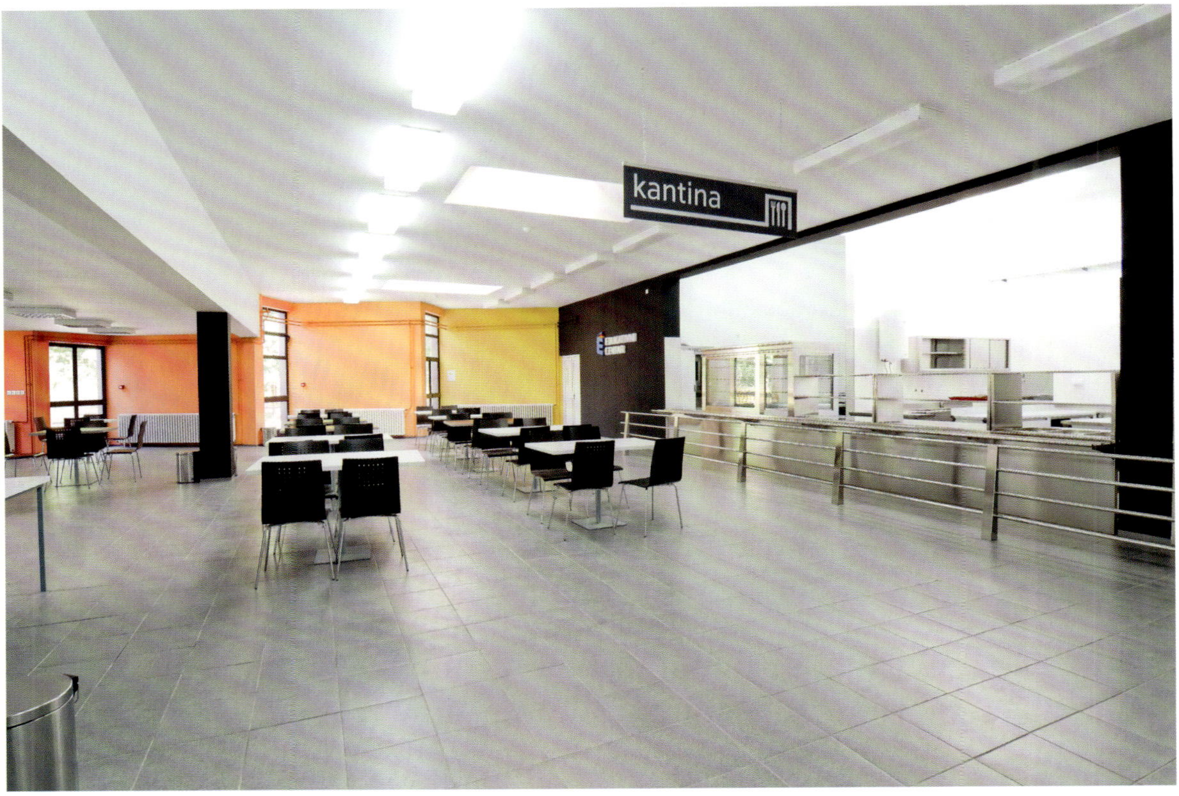
kantina

Kindergarten and crèche Prangins

The new Prangins kindergarten is conceived as one big house that has been placed on a sloping site. The cruciform structure resulting from the interlocking volumes allow it to have a special relationship with the neighbouring ensemble. The four volumes, which are mutually staggered by a third of each unit's floor height and interleaved, make the building appear to be smaller and visually less obtrusive.

The six classrooms are organised in groups of two and occupy the three lower volumes. Due to its central location, the staircase is a fundamental, structuring element of the kindergarten. The ramps that accompany it provide parallel access and act as an internal entrance to the crèche. The volume of the crèche, which is placed perpendicular to the first wing, marks and covers the entrance area of the kindergarten. Direct access to the upper part of the property also enables independent operation of the crèche. The crèche floor plan consists of a large (dining) room, which can be divided into several smaller units according to requirements.

The natural qualities of the location are highlighted by the different alignment of the large window openings, since the design paid great attention to visual relationships with respect to their placement. The reinforced concrete that is visible both inside and outside, anchors the building into the topography.

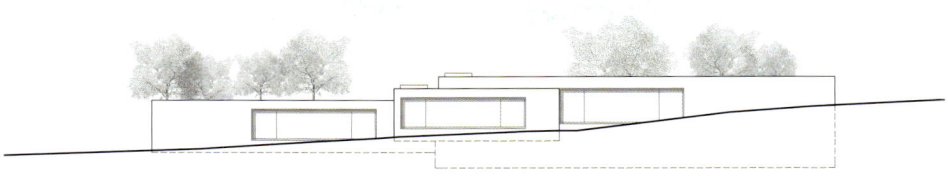

NORTH-EAST ELEVATION

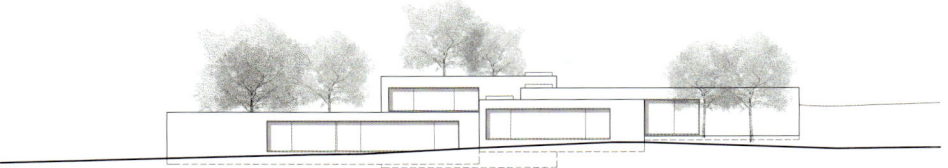

SOUTH-EAST ELEVATION

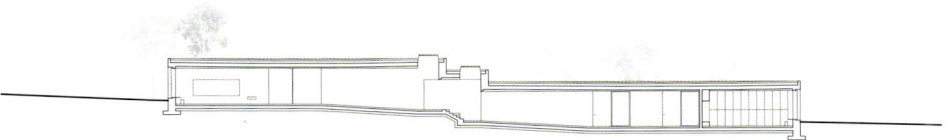

CLASSROOM SECTION

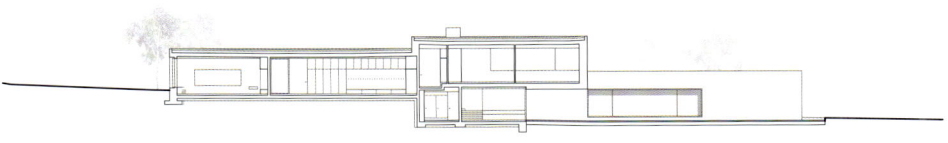

ENTRANCE HALL SECTION

0   5   10   20

Architects : Pierre-Alain Dupraz
Country : Switzerland
Design Agency :
PIERRE-ALAIN DUPRAZ ARCHITECTE ETS FAS
Photographer : Thomas Jantscher
Fernando Guerra, Samuele Evolvi
Client : Commune de Prangins
Project Location : Prangins, Vaud, Switzerland

Kindergarten and crèche Prangins

Architects : Pierre-Alain Dupraz
Country : Switzerland

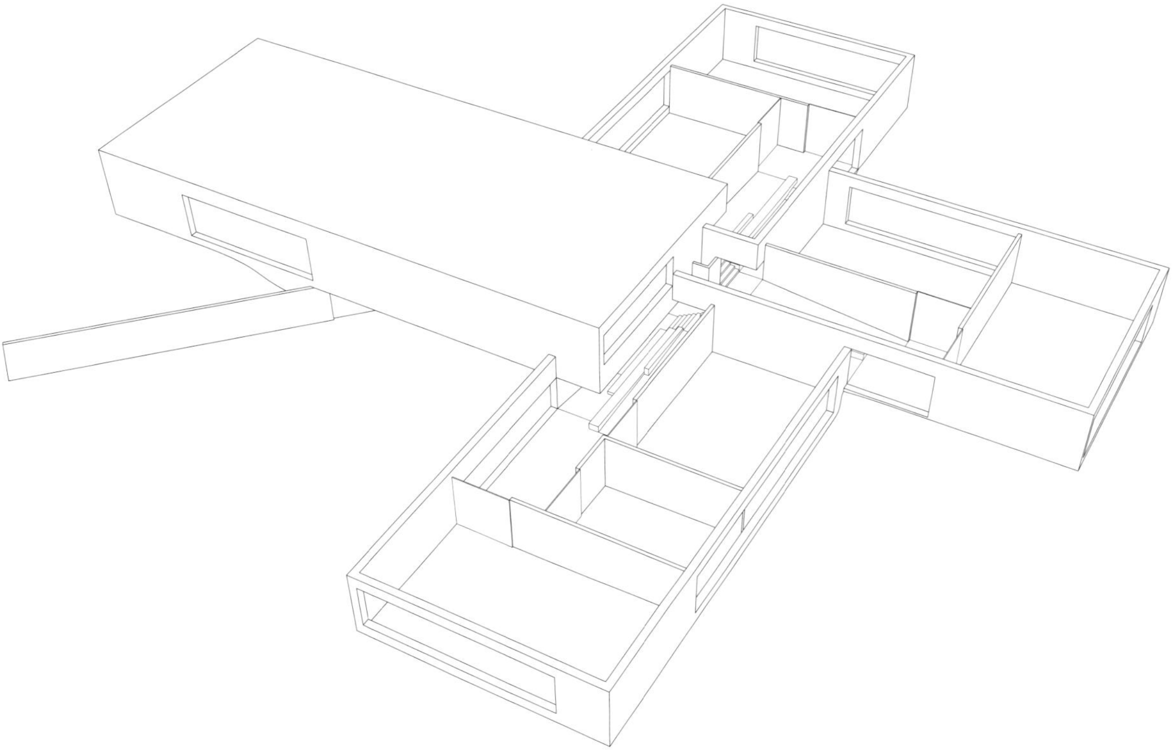

Kindergarten and crèche Prangins

Architects : Pierre-Alain Dupraz
Country : Switzerland

Kindergarten and crèche Prangins

Architects : Pierre-Alain Dupraz
Country : Switzerland

Kindergarten and crèche Prangins

Architects : Pierre-Alain Dupraz
Country : Switzerland

Kindergarten and crèche Prangins

Architects : Pierre-Alain Dupraz
Country : Switzerland

Kindergarten and crèche Prangins

Architects : Pierre-Alain Dupraz
Country : Switzerland

Kindergarten and crèche Prangins

Architects : Pierre-Alain Dupraz
Country : Switzerland

Architects : Rh+ architecture
Country : France
Photographer : Luc Boegly
Total surface area : 1800m²
Client : City of Paris
Project Location : Paris 13e

Early childhood education center

The project is built on a continuous base to harmonize the street and bring a subtle plastic richness. The buildings above are implemented so in order to follow the slope of the street and space out to avoid creating built facades.

This decomposed volumetry, on a domestic scale, allows a delicate insertion and clears out generous external spaces with multiple perspectives for all, occupants and neighbors.

Visual relations at the heart of this ancient homogeneous islet are thus preserved.

Early childhood education center

Architects : Rh+ architecture
Country : France

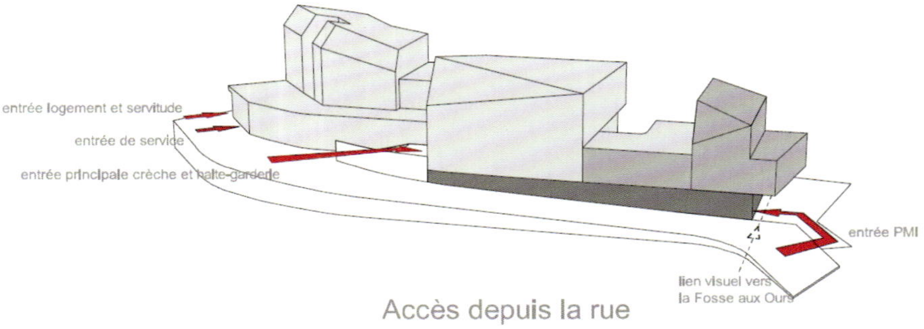

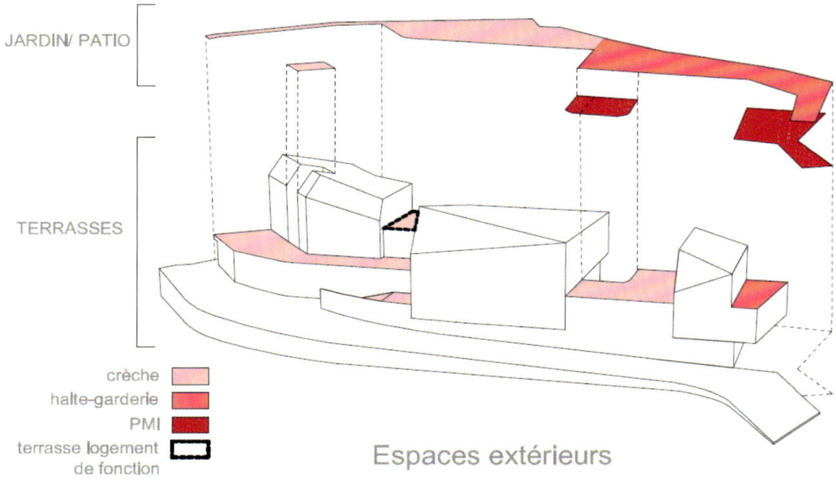

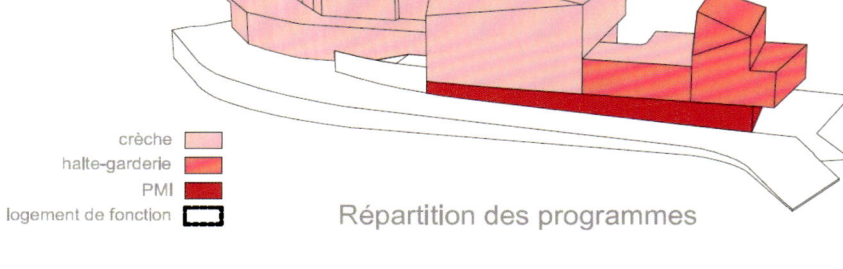

Early childhood education center

． ． ． ．

Architects : Rh+ architecture
Country : France

Early childhood education center

Architects : Rh+ architecture
Country : France

54

Early childhood education center

Architects : Rh+ arch tecture
Country : France

Early childhood education center

Architects : Rh+ architecture
Country : France

Architects : Maria José Pizarro, Óscar Rueda
Country : Spain
Design Agency : Rueda Pizarro Architects SLP
Photographer : Miguel de Guzmán
Total surface area : 1500m²
Client : City of Leganés
Project Location : C / Zamora. Leganés, Madrid

Kindergarten in Students' Path, Leganés. Madrid

Parallelism with the famous novel "Alice in Wonderland" by Lewis Carroll is immediate. It transports us to a world of mixed feelings where imagination and reality, work and play, fun and responsibility are combined. A world of sensations, experiences, sets of scales and color are perceived by the eyes of children, coexisting with adults, making necessary to use a dual scale adapted to each of them. But not only the scale must be adapted, also the space perception. Due to this reason, we consider essential thinking from inside the building. First of all, the central space works as a public space covered where you can access to all classrooms. It is a smooth space with items that enhance visual and tactile perception: the circular courtyard, that introduces outside to inside; the deep cover skylights larger than 2 meters of height that introduce a world of color; the access to the classrooms with partitions unfolded and deep windows that work as a individual spaces and allow to the children enter inside. These are resources that enhance haptic space against a purely visual space.

The layout of the program inside the school attends to circulation and orientation criteria. The classrooms are located in the southeast to get the most sunlight. The administration, offices and facilities are located in the northwest where movement and access are independent. The main space is the great central hall, a covered meeting space for children's events that allows direct access to all classrooms.

Kindergarten in Students' Path, Leganés. Madrid

Architects : Maria José Pizarro, Óscar Rueda
Country : Spain

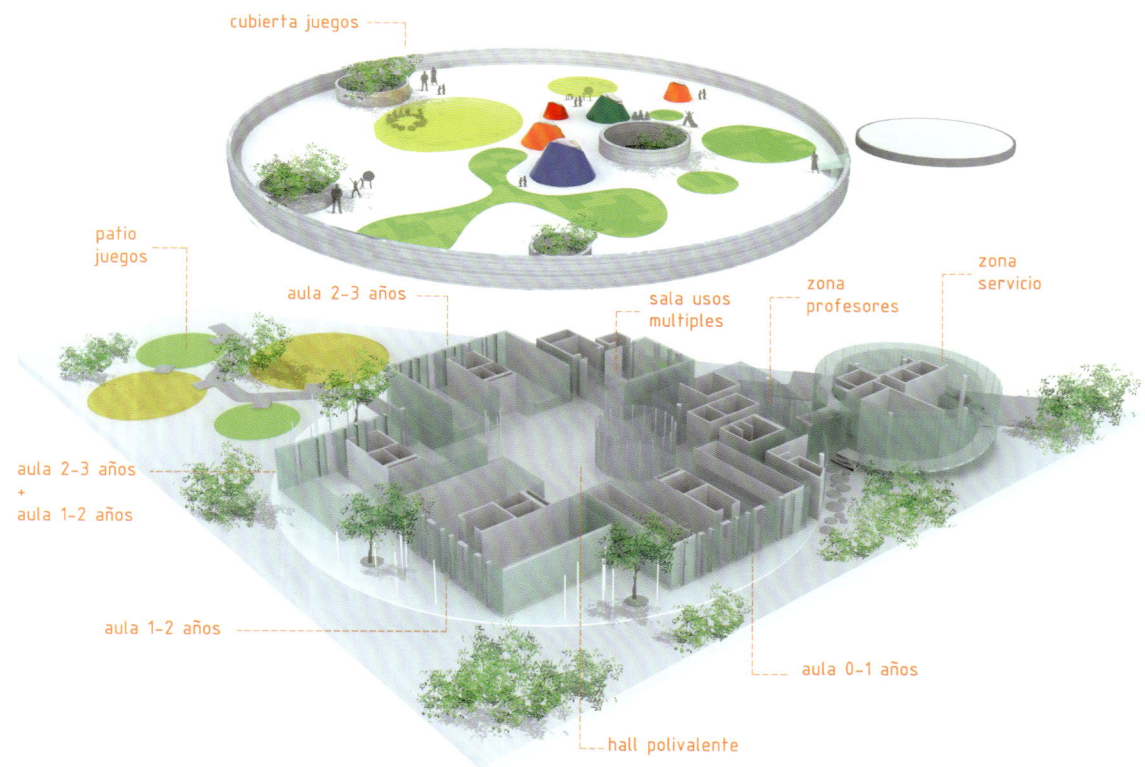

Kindergarten in Students' Path, Leganés. Madrid

Architects : María José Pizarro, Óscar Rueda
Country : Spain

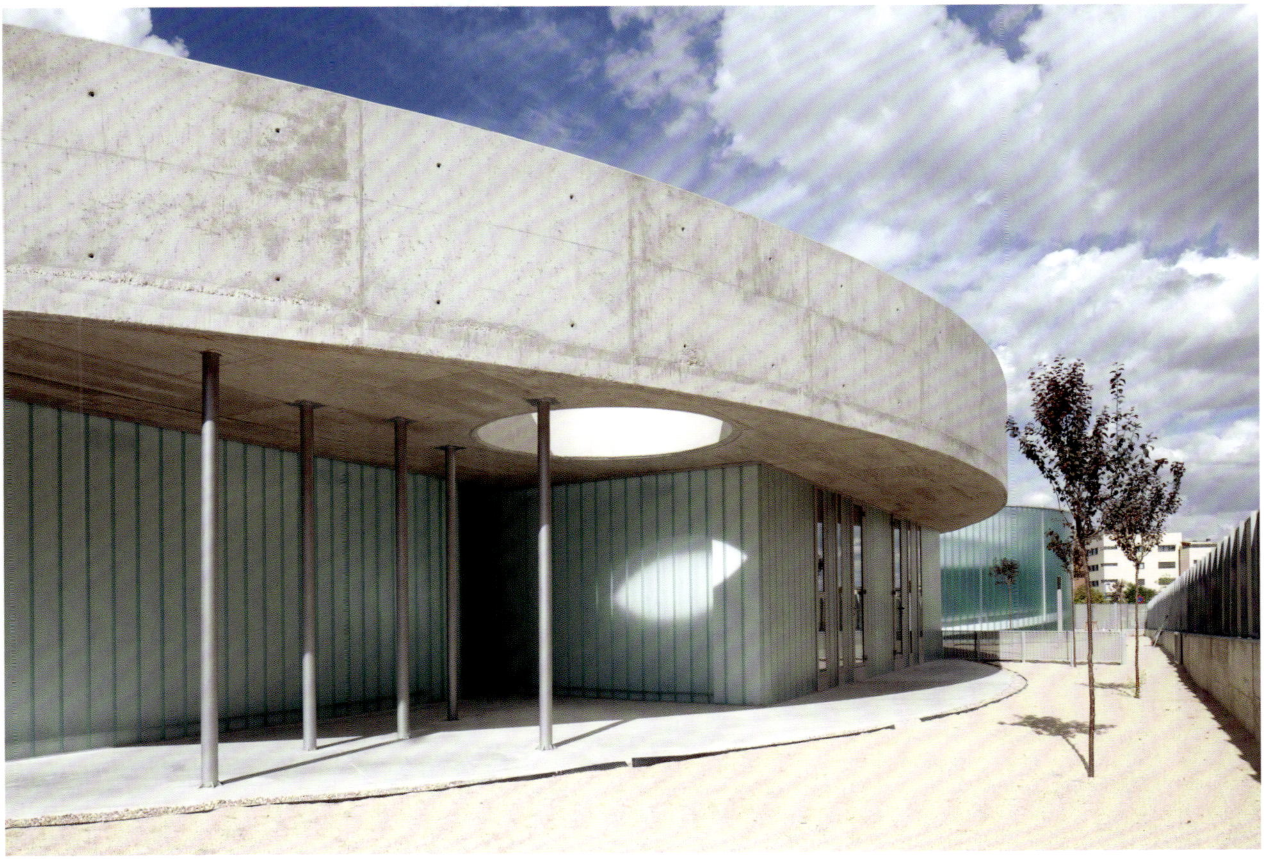

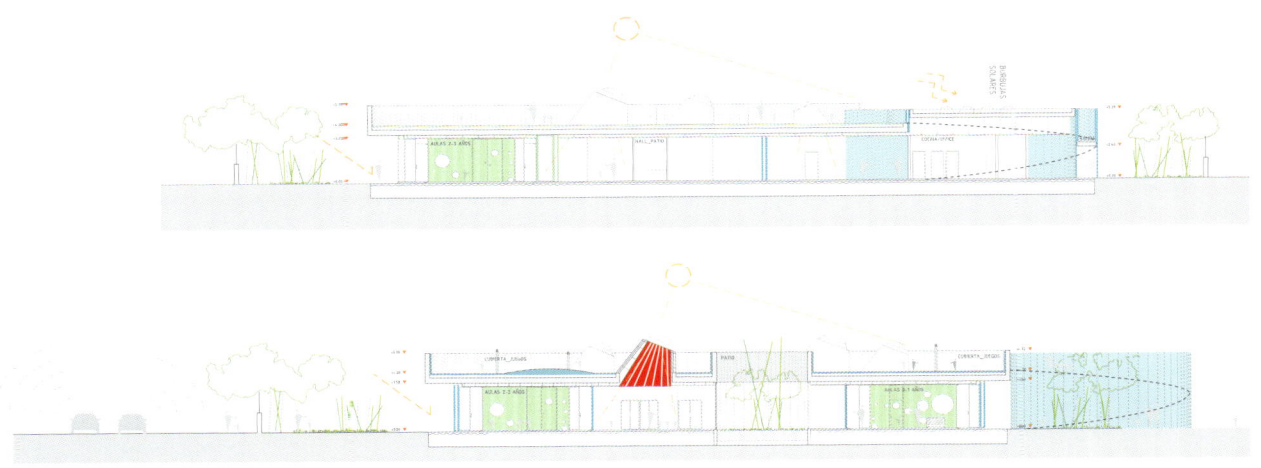

Kindergarten in Students' Path, Leganés. Madrid

Architects : María José Pizarro, Óscar Rueda
Country : Spain

Kindergarten in Students' Path, Leganés. Madrid

Architects : María José Pizarro, Óscar Rueda
Country : Spain

Tetris Nursery

As for the programs of learning diverse experiences for kids, we tried to introduce various spatial events which are continued by strolling all around the places in this kindergarten. From playground, through the playstair, rest terrace, playbridge, roof-playstair, upto roofgarden, there are various strolling spaces of circulation and playful spaces.

Consequently, all the inner and outer spaces are playful spaces, at the same time, they are the places of learning diverse experiences, we expected this kindergarten to be the educational places for various experiences of many kinds of qualities of spaces. To introduce southern sunlight, we adapted clearstory system to each roofs of this kindergarten, so it divided into several masses which look like Tetris block. By design the colorful glazed windows of translucence, we tried to teach all kids the physical experiences of change of color and mixed color.

We expect all the parts of this architecture could be the learning things for all the kids of this kindergarten.

Architects : HyoMan Kim
Country : Korea

Tetris Nursery

Architects : HyoMan Kim
Country : Korea

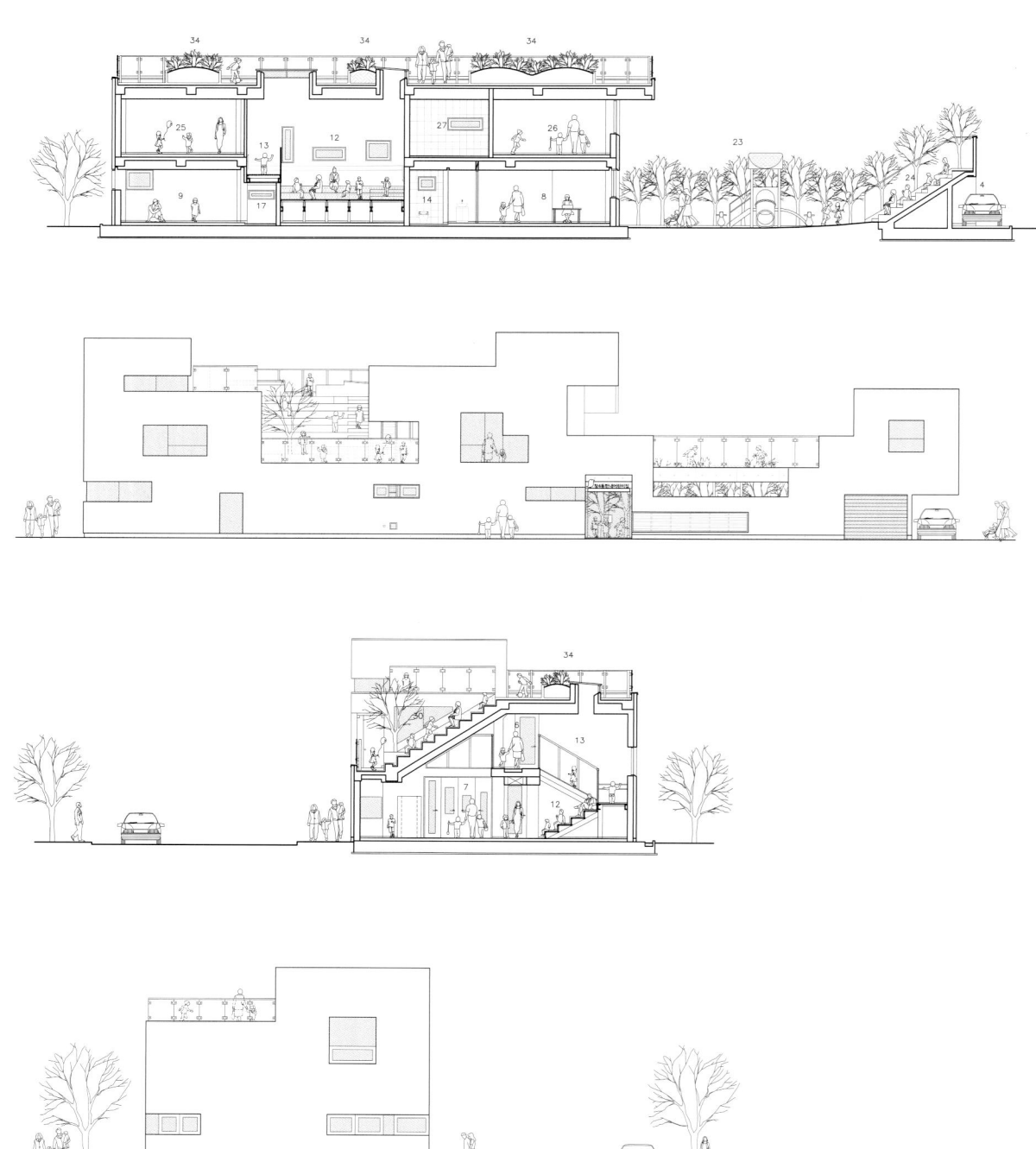

Tetris Nursery

Architects : HyoMan Kim
Country : Korea

74

Tetris Nursery

Architects : HyoMan Kim
Country : Korea

Tetris Nursery

Architects : HyoMan Kim
Country : Korea

77

Architects : Hirotani Yoshihiro, Ishida Yusaku,
Archivision Hirotani Studio
Country : Japan

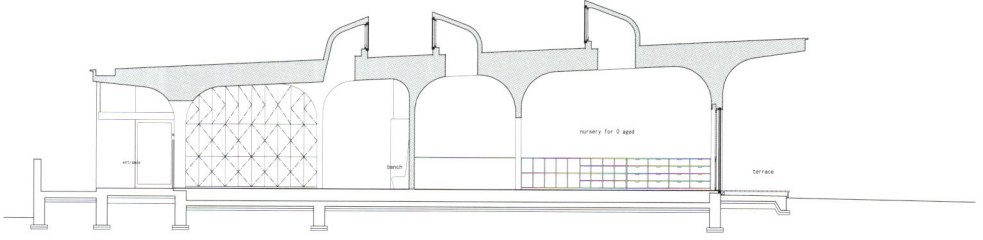

Leimond-Shonaka Nursery School

This is about a nursery facility for 140 children ranging from ages zero to five years in Asahi city, within Owari district, Aichi prefecture. In the past, in many nursery facilities, the daily activities of the children such as playing, eating, going to the bathroom or sleeping were done in various divided functional rooms.

Whereas, our aim is to capture these activities of the children within a continuous time mode, and within this time receptacle, to lay out the architecture and the plotted artwork, working together to create a nursery facility likened to a three-dimensional picture book.

For this reason, we have reverted to using the technique of overlapping in order to separately sequester a design to impress the functional form of the floor plan and the image of the entire space.

Leimond-Shonaka Nursery School

Architects : Hirotani Yosh hiro, Ishida Yusaku,
Archivision Hirotani Studio
Country : Japan

Leimond-Shonaka Nursery School

Architects : Hirotani Yoshihiro, Ishida Yusaku,
Archivision Hirotani Studio
Country : Japan

Leimond-Shonaka Nursery School
● ● ● ●

Architects : Hirotani Yoshihiro, Ishida Yusaku,
Archivision Hirotani Studio
Country : Japan

Leimond-Shonaka Nursery School

Architects : Hirotani Yoshihiro, Ishida Yusaku,
Archivision Hirotani Studio
Country : Japan

Leimond-Shonaka Nursery School

Architects : Hirotani Yoshihiro, Ishida Yusaku,
Archivision Hirotani Studio
Country : Japan

Leimond-Shonaka Nursery School

Architects : Hirotani Yoshihiro, Ishida Yusaku,
Archivision Hirotani Studio
Country : Japan

Architects : Kentaro Yamazaki
Country : Japan
Design Agency : Yamazaki Kentaro Design Workshop
Photographer : Naoomi Kurozumi

Hakusui Nursery School

This nursery school in Sakura, Chiba was planned to accommodate 60 pupils.

Seiyu-Kai, a local social welfare firm specializing in elderly care facilities approached us for this project. The overarching concept for this plan started with an idea : "a nursery school is a large house." Surrounded by mountains and forest, the southern area of the site rests on a gentle slope. Putting this topography to use, we designed the school room to resemble a large set of stairs.

Our goal was to create a space that was not only fun for the children but via blending into the nature around it, foster an experience that was greater than the sum of its elements.he entire space.

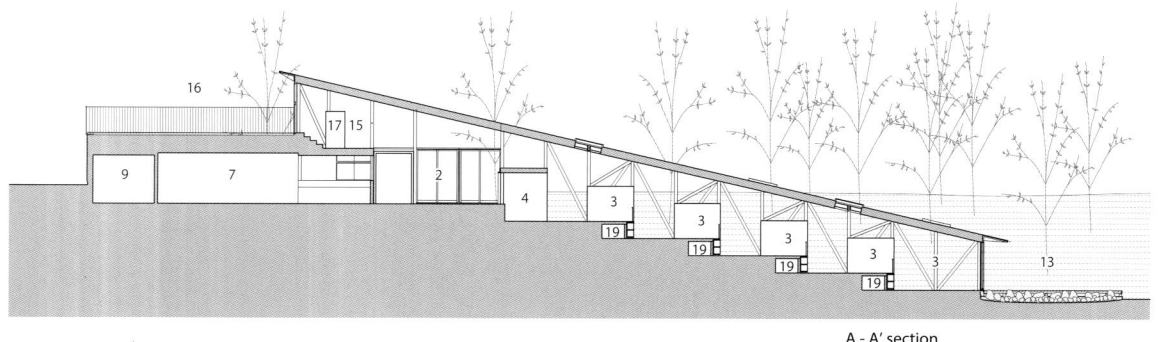

A - A' section

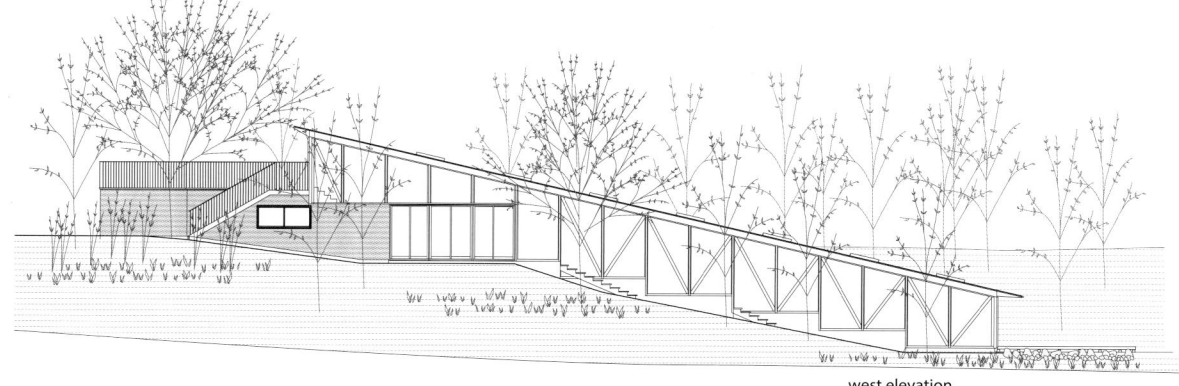

west elevation

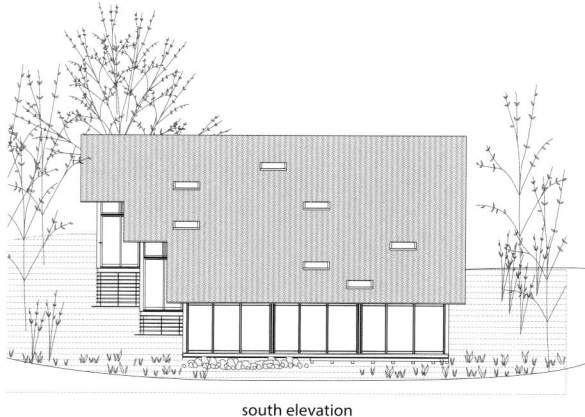

B - B' section

south elevation

0 1 2 3 5

Hakusui Nursery School

Architects : Kentaro Yamazaki
Country : Japan

Hakusui Nursery School

Architects : Kentaro Yamazaki
Country : Japan

Hakusui Nursery School

Architects : Kentaro Yamazaki
Country : Japan

Hakusui Nursery School

Architects : Kentaro Yamazaki
Country : Japan

IKC ZevenZeeën

* * * *

In Banne Buiksloot in the north of Amsterdam the general building fabric consists of high apartment blocks. In contrast the public buildings do the opposite. They form a network of low buildings that seek a strong connection to the public domain. The new 2 storey primary school, designed by the architect Gianni Cito of the Amsterdam office Moke Architecten, does the same. The school stands out due to its crenelated shed roof and the tribune stairway that connects the school with the playground. The playful round windows and the red scaly facade give the building an autonomous expression that fits its public role.

An IKC is an integral kids centre and it offers a place for kids from 0 until 12 and for their parents. Besides the school the building also accommodates a childcare centre and a parents room. The wide corricors with calm colours suit the educational philosophy of the Dalton school. The school strongly relies on individual initiative of its pupils. It offers a large variety of working places for individual and group work. The use of wood for the window frames between the corridor and the classrooms, the ceiling and all integrated cabinets strengthens the soft and natural expression of the interior. Both cabinets and ceiling have a noise-reducing surface.

The building is one of the first completely energy neutral schools in the Netherlands. The double prefab concrete facade in combination with high spaces and predominantly northern light, strongly reduce the warming up of the spaces during daytime. During the nights the room temperature drops in a natural way. Therefor the building is cooled naturally, which reduces the use of energy. The shed roof is covered with 324 PV-panels.

Architects : Gianni Cito
Country : Nederland
Design Agency : Moke Architecten
Team : P. de Weerd, V. Falconi, N. Leszczynska
Photographer : Thijs Wolzak
Dimensions : 2000m²
Client : City of Amsterdam Noord
Structural engineer : Pieters Bouwtechniek
Environmental engineer : Merosch
Quantity surveyor : Boshuizen Bouwadvies
Project Location : Amsterdam, the Netherlands

IKC ZevenZeeën

Architects : Gianni Cito
Country : Nederland

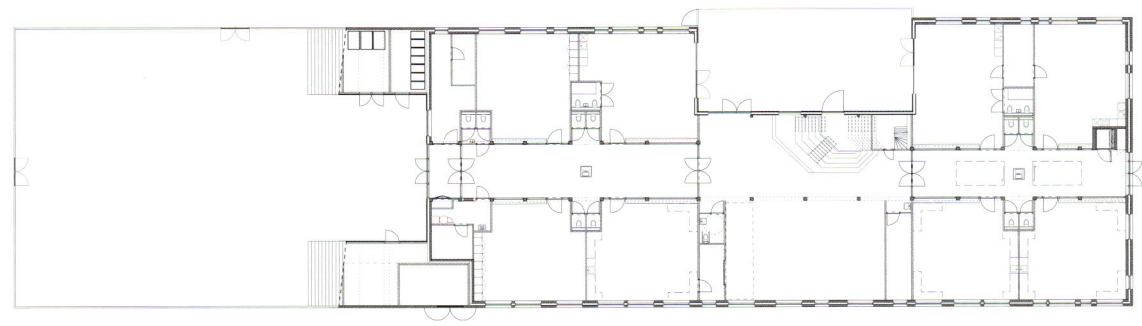

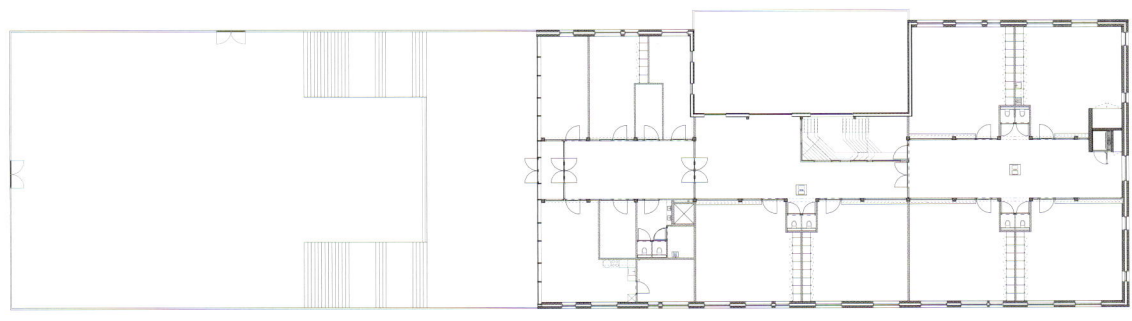

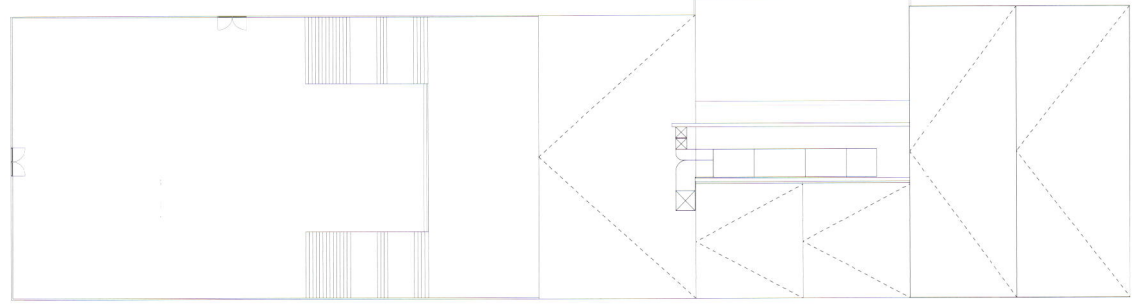

IKC ZevenZeeën

Architects : Gianni Cito
Country   Nederland

IKC ZevenZeeën

Architects : Gianni Cito
Country : Nederland

IKC ZevenZeeën

Architects : Gianni Cito
Country : Nederland

IKC ZevenZeeën

Architects : Gianni Cito
Country : Nederland

IKC ZevenZeeën

* * * *

Architects : Gianni Cito
Country : Nederland

116

east elevation

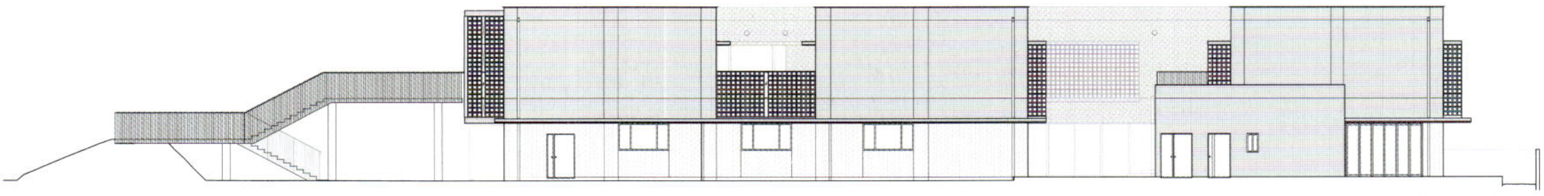

west elevation

HZ Kindergarten and Nursery

This site is located in Miyakojima where it's about 2000 km away from Tokyo in Japan to the southwest. Miyakojima belongs to a subtropical oceanic climate and is surrounded by blue sea and coral reef, and the island where Ryukyu limestone rose. The Building is required to close for making shade and also open for ventilation, because of the environment that hotness and humid by many typhoon attack.

This plan was made strongly against typhoon and shut out the sunlight by leading with the construction through which a wind blows.

We planned the space locate in the first floor that is public, a studio and an atelier for the creative activity which attached great importance to bringing up creativity of the childhood, and dining for food education. And childcare room and picture book corner locate in the second floor that is private. Take advantage of this thin site, the first floor placed playground- studio- atelier- courtyard- dining continuous and it became one large space and wind blows through when open windows.

It's based on traditional wooden red roofing tile architecture seen in this area The structure is steel reinforced concrete construction that endure a typhoon invasion.

Around outer perimeter of the building, low canopies and screen made by concrete blocks with a holes which is original building material in this area protect from flying objects and shut out the sunlight through keep view and wind. The color of the outer wall tile was chosen the one which is similar to the traditional red roof tile color and it would blend into the region.

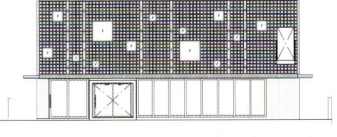
north elevation

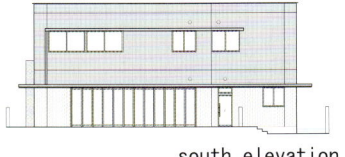
south elevation

Design Agency :
HIBINOSEKKEI + Youji no Shiro (www.e-ensha.com)
Country : Japan
Site area : 1846.56m²
Surface area : 596.58m²
Building area : 1107.56m²
Photography : Studio Bauhaus, Ryuji Inoue
Project Location : Okinawa, Japan

Detail of concrete blocks screen

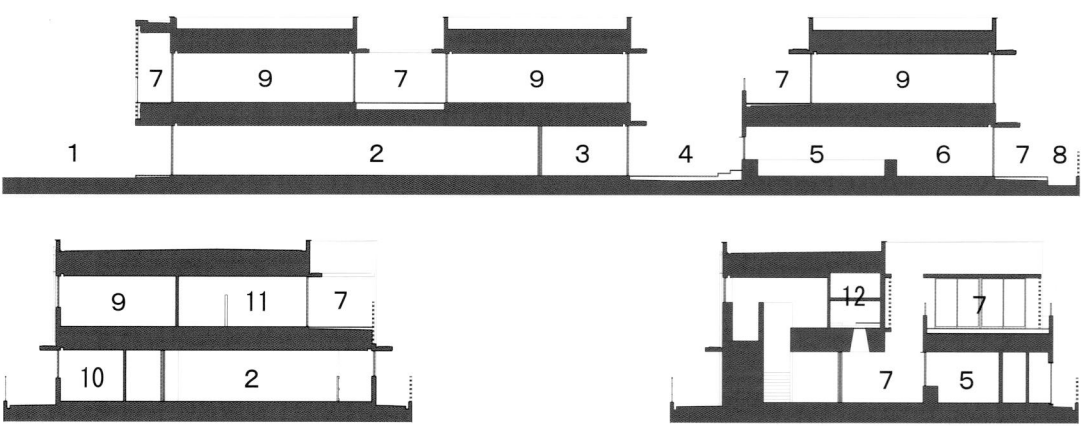

Section

1. play ground
2. studio
3. atelier
4. courtyard
5. kitchen
6. dining
7. terrace
8. dining garden
9. childcare room
10. ofiice
11. toilet
12. small playroom

HZ Kindergarten and Nursery

Architects : HIBINOSEKKEI + Youji no Shiro
Country : Japan

120

HZ Kindergarten and Nursery

Architects : HIBINOSEKKEI + Youji no Shiro
Country : Japan

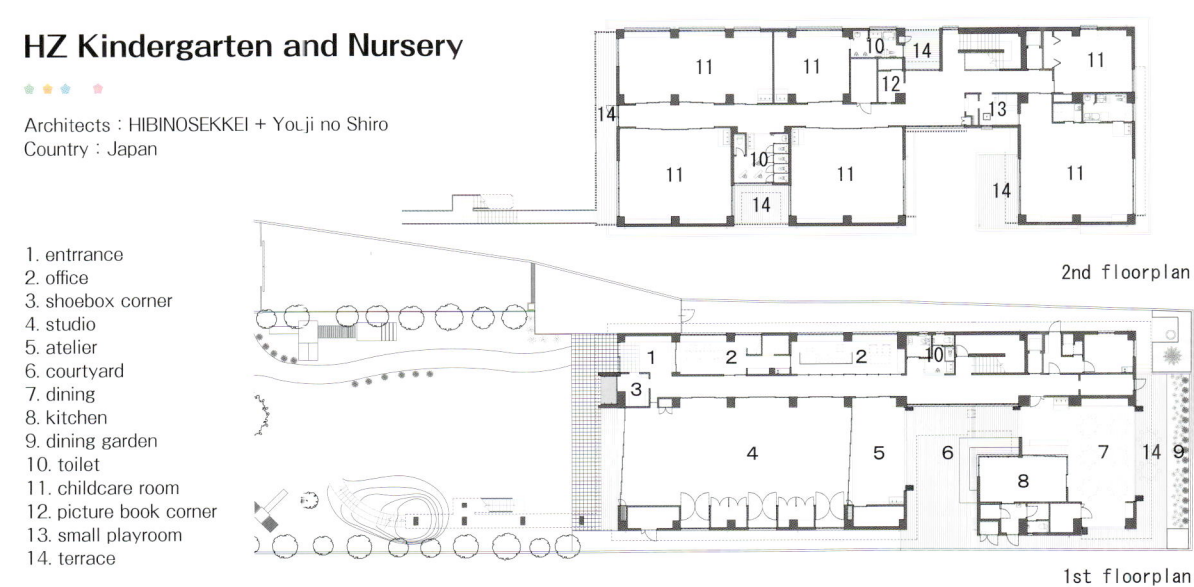

HZ Kindergarten and Nursery

⭐⭐⭐⭐

Architects : HIBINOSEKKEI + Youji no Shiro
Country : Japan

1. entrrance
2. office
3. shoebox corner
4. studio
5. atelier
6. courtyard
7. dining
8. kitchen
9. dining garden
10. toilet
11. childcare room
12. picture book corner
13. small playroom
14. terrace

HZ Kindergarten and Nursery

Architects : HIBINOSEKKEI + Youji no Shiro
Country : Japan

126

HZ Kindergarten and Nursery

Architects : HIBINOSEKKEI + Youji no Shiro
Country : Japan

D1 Kindergarten and Nursery

We plan not to set a partition in nursery room and partition off by furniture where they can change form and territory of the class at their discretion. We made a system where the children purchase the furniture when they enter the kindergarten and bring it home when they graduate. By this system, they can keep their kindergarten clean since the furniture is renewed by 1 academic year every year.

As form of the furniture can be also changed when it is renewed, the furniture is also changeable. Tategu (fixture that partitions off building such as door, sliding door, window frame, etc.) can open the whole building, and thereby they can use the whole building as a space half outside, which provides a space with high freedom. They can avoid strong sunlight and light rain since screen for outside is set at outside of the building.

As roof of piloti can be opened and closed by weather, it can be used for stadium for all weather such as badminton, volleyball and other sport. Other than that, as it can be a lunch room by cooperating with neighboring kitchen, they can use inside space as outside space by opening the roof and tetegu. This kind of highly free space, which is used for all purposes, creates many types of play area stimulating the children's creativity.

Design Agency :
HIBINOSEKKEI + Youji no Shiro (www.e-ensha.com)
Country : Japan
Site area : 3084.57m²
Surface area : 1213.26m²
Building area : 1161.63m²
Photography : Studio Bauhaus, Ryuji Inoue
Project Location : Kimamoto, Japan

D1 Kindergarten and Nursery

* * * *

Architects : HIBINOSEKKEI + Youji no Shiro
Country : Japan

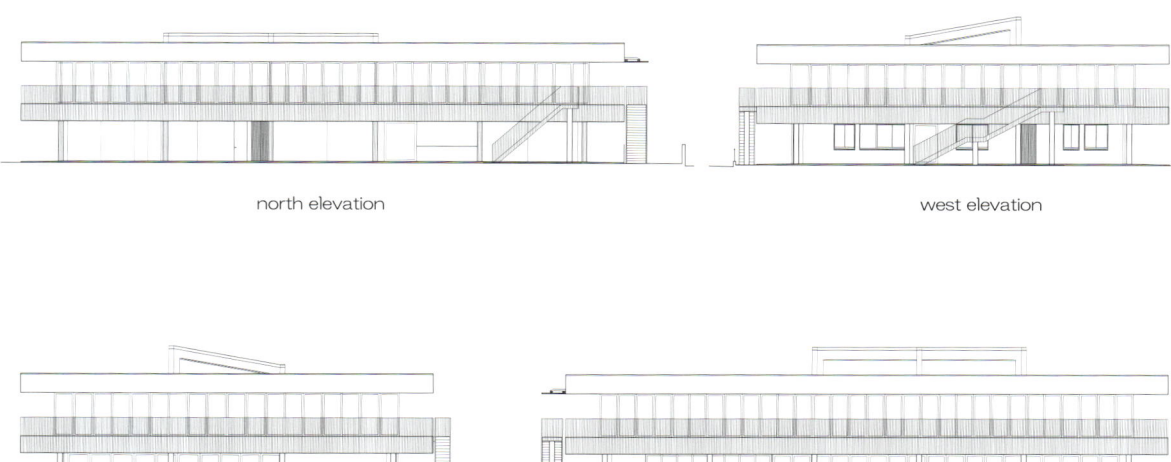

north elevation

west elevation

east elevation

south elevation

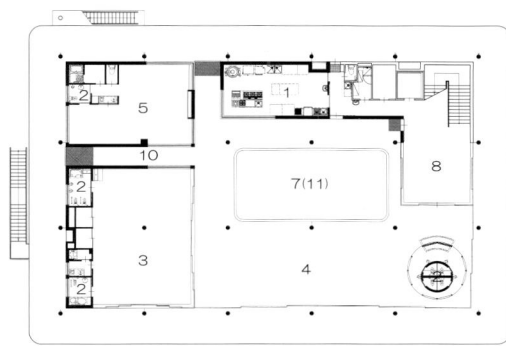
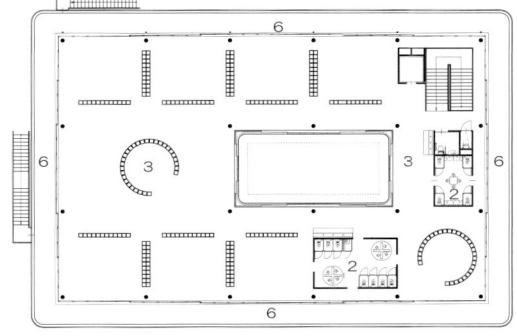

1st floorplan

2nd floorplan

1. kitchen
2. toilet
3. childcare room
4. piloti
5. ofiice
6. balcony

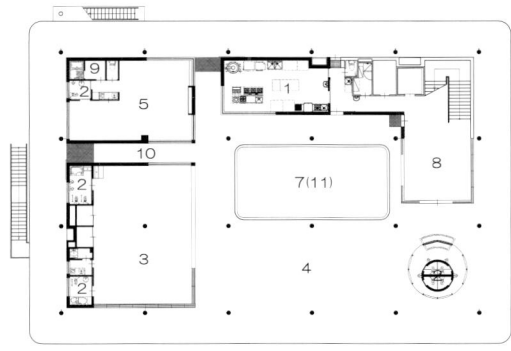
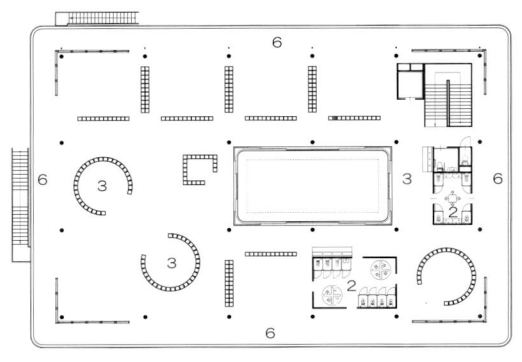

1st floorplan

2nd floorplan

7. countyard
8. entrance
9. dressing room
10. passage
11. basin

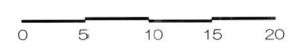

D1 Kindergarten and Nursery

⭐ ⭐ ⭐ ⭐

Architects：HIBINOSEKKEI + Youji no Shiro
Country：Japan

133

D1 Kindergarten and Nursery

Architects : HIBINOSEKKEI + Youji no Shiro
Country : Japan

DS Nursery

The site is surrounded by rice field where wind blows through well. This is one of the areas with much quantity of wind-generated electricity in Japan, and this project is based on the concept of "wind".

Planning is layout corridor of the ring shape as an image that wind around and each room volume as blade of the windmill. Consequently, even while maintaining the independence, there is a sense of unity through the corridor and courtyard. And it secures natural lighting and ventilation by the opening of the high-side windows of classrooms and playroom, and windows of the corridor, which is not to depend on the machine.

It is timber and one-story building, and it has low canopies outer perimeter of the building. There is a wood deck terrace under the canopy, and it is possible to use as semi-outdoor space by a large opening of the classroom. Where children use is shown the timber beams and it expresses that it is timber building. Even out of those, lunch room is created a state close to the natural environment by timber fitting of large opening and terrace connect with full of green courtyard. Children enjoy lunchtime in this comfortable space. The green courtyard can be see and accessed from any place is planned as a place where children create play and discover small from various planting. In addition, there is a children's toilet with a large glass window face to the courtyard. It is bright and fun space that children want to go. There is also an effect that does not smell by ultraviolet rays that enters always.

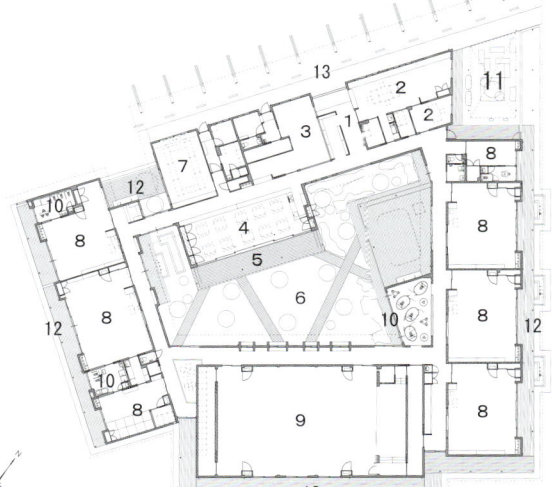

1. entrance
2. ofiice
3. kitchen
4. lunchroom
5. lunch terrace
6. courtyard
7. conference room
8. childcare room
9. playroom
10. toilet
11. playcorner
12. terrace
13. piloti

Design Agency :
HIBINOSEKKEI + Youji no Shiro (www.e-ensha.com)
Country : Japan
Site area : 7179.41m²
Surface area : 1710.22m²
Building area : 1464.90m²
Photography : Studio Bauhaus, Ryuji Inoue

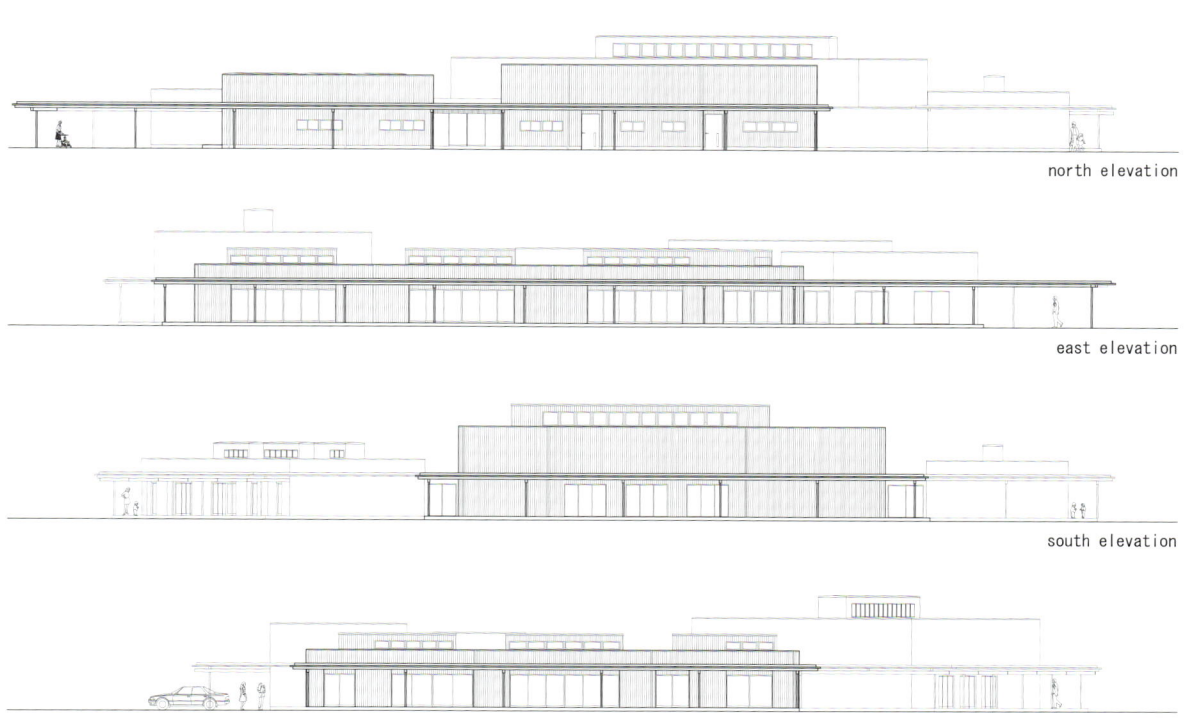

north elevation

east elevation

south elevation

west elevation

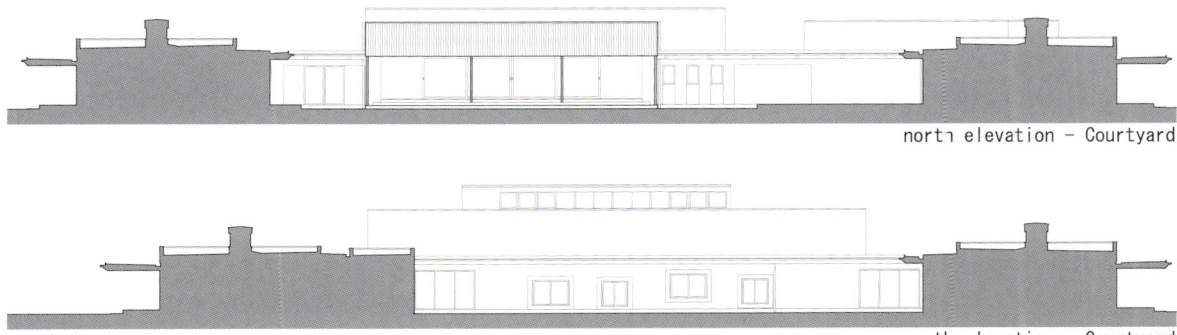

north elevation - Courtyard

south elevation - Courtyard

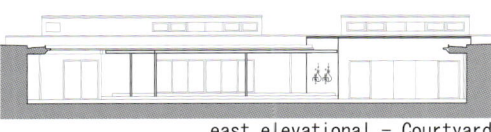

east elevational - Courtyard

west elevation - Courtyard

DS Nursery

* * * *

Architects : HIBINOSEKKEI + Youji no Shiro
Country : Japan

DS Nursery

Architects : HIBINOSEKKEI + Youji no Shiro
Country : Japan

DS Nursery

● ● ● ●

Architects : HIBINOSEKKEI + Youji no Shiro
Country : Japan

ST Nursery

The whole structure is designed to naturally promote direct and indirect interaction even while being engaged with some other activity. It is a learning environment to develop communication and consideration towards others. The overall form looks like small huts arranged along the riverside, an attempt to bring back an old scene of this area from long time back, an open experience is created at just beside the main entrance where you are allowed to relax without taking off your shoes, to create the look and feel of the old riverside cafe.

The roofs are interconnected and have slope in accordance to the climatology and spatial function. The irregularity of the ceiling height thus invites children's curiosity. The space created by connecting the small huts is used as patio while that in between becoming the age wise play gardens. The width of patio is decided in accordance to maintaining privacy while still establishing the visual link amongst the kids inside and outside. Toilet, library, dining room and infant nursery all are linked with the patio as their mediator.

This nursery isn't just about promoting the communication in between the children but everyone including the teachers.

Design Agency :
HIBINOSEKKEI + Youji no Shiro (www.e-ensha.com)
Country : Japan
Site area : 3111.99m²
Surface area : 882.90m²
Building area : 768.74m²
Photography : Studio Bauhaus, Ryuji Inoue

Elevation

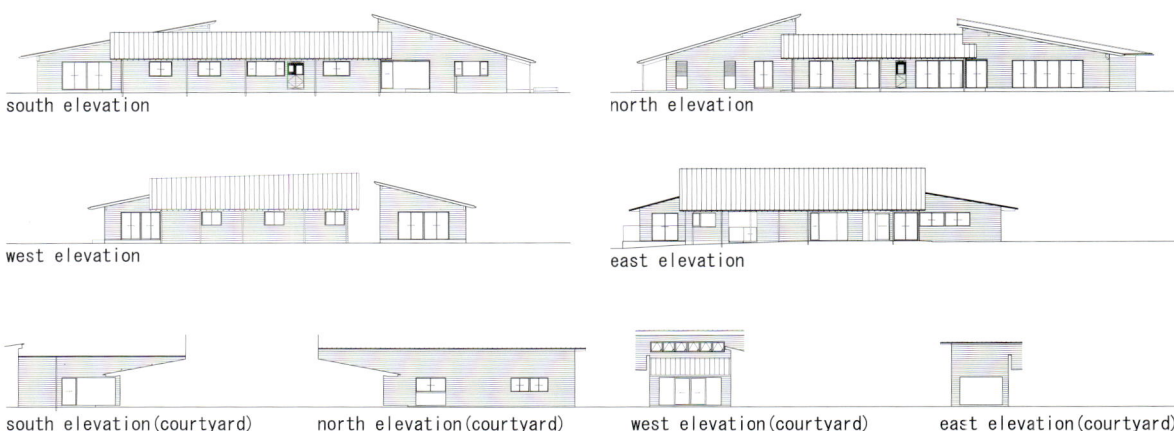

south elevation

north elevation

west elevation

east elevation

south elevation (courtyard)

north elevation (courtyard)

west elevation (courtyard)

east elevation (courtyard)

ST Nursery

● ● ● ●

Architects : HIBINOSEKKEI + Youji no Shiro
Country : Japan

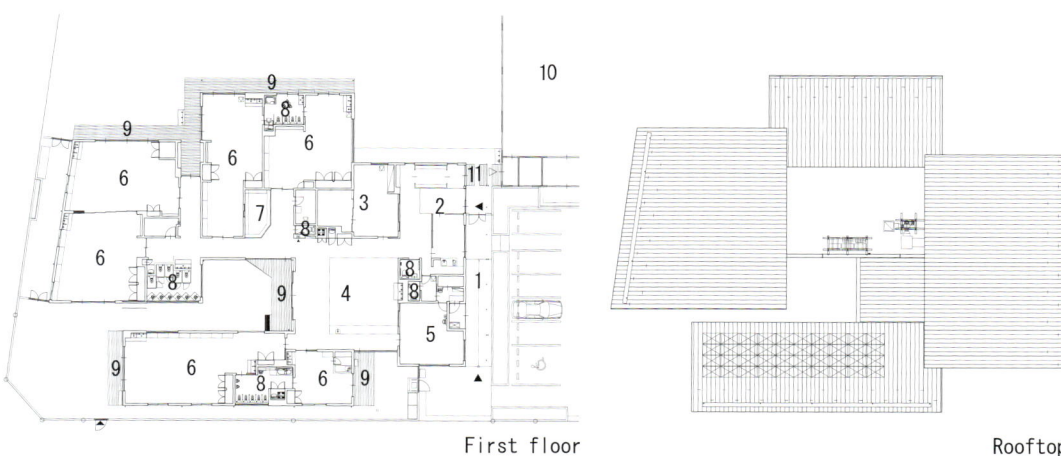

First floor　　　　　　　　　　Rooftop

1. approach
2. entrance hall
3. office
4. dining room
5. kitchen
6. childcare room
7. library
8. restroom
9. play terrace
10. play hall
11. corridor

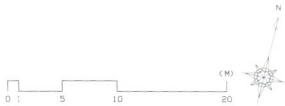

ST Nursery

Architects : HIBINOSEKKEI + Youji no Shiro
Country : Japan

1. parking
2. play hall
3. play ground
4. courtyard

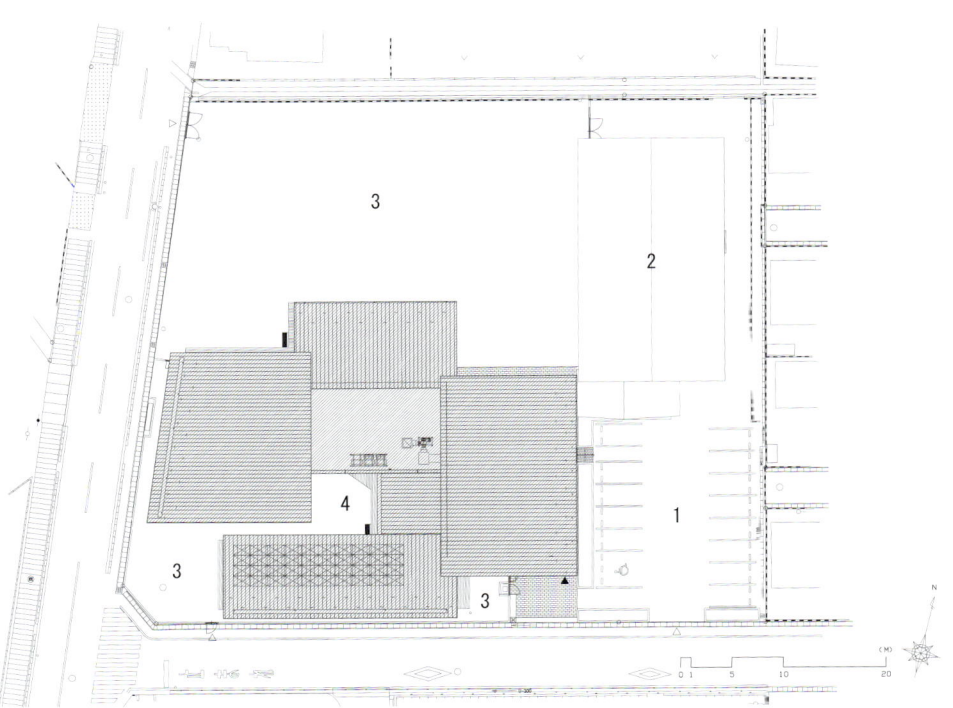

150

ST Nursery

Architects : HIBINOSEKKEI + Youji no Shiro
Country : Japan

ST Nursery

Architects : HIBINOSEKKEI + Youji no Shiro
Country : Japan

TY Nursery

It is an area surrounded by sufficient nature with green where you can feel change of season such as field, pond, forest, woods and others, and in addition, comfortable wind blows.

For those who live in this area, the field, pond and trees they can see from the site are not special but close to them. The change of the nature they can feel by season teaches children variable facts throughout a year. In summer, water spreads in the field, trees turn red in autumn, snow falls in winter and flowers start blooming in spring. In this project, we emphasized that this scenery they feel naturally is input into the body of the children deeply and they learn by experience.

In dining room, a large window is set at two phases where they can see the scenery such as the field and pond. By this setting, they can enjoy eating while seeing change of the scenery throughout a year. At front, a terrace is set, and they can have lunch by feeling sunlight and wind at their skin as if they were having a picnic on nice day. To stimulate imagination of the children, in the hall, we set a light at random as if it were constellation they can see from here. By discovering the constellation by themselves and teaching each other, they develop joy of discovery, mind of searching and curiosity. A device of accumulating water is designed on top of the terrace in the hall, and cooled air is brought into the building by using vaporization heat. On hot days in summer, it is used as an Ashimizu (putting foot in the water to cool down) where they can have fun, and thereby they can live without relying on air conditioner.

As a place for developing an area and establishing a community, we created a place where raising of the children is supported. Its purpose is not only to reduce stress of child care of the parent who has a problem in raising children but also mothers and those in the area can communicate each other easily. The space as if it were an open café lounge makes visitors feel relaxed and provides an environment where they can easily consult.

In the garden, a variety of trees such as the one producing fruit are planted. They bring this fruit to the kitchen, cook it by themselves and eat. By this experience, they develop sensitivity, curiosity and mind of searching.

Design Agency :
HIBINOSEKKEI + Youji no Shiro (www.e-ensha.com)
Country : Japan
Site area : 4529.83m²
Surface area : 846.57m²
Building area : 1242.37m²
Photography : Studio Bauhaus, Ryuji Inoue
Project Location : Mie, Japan

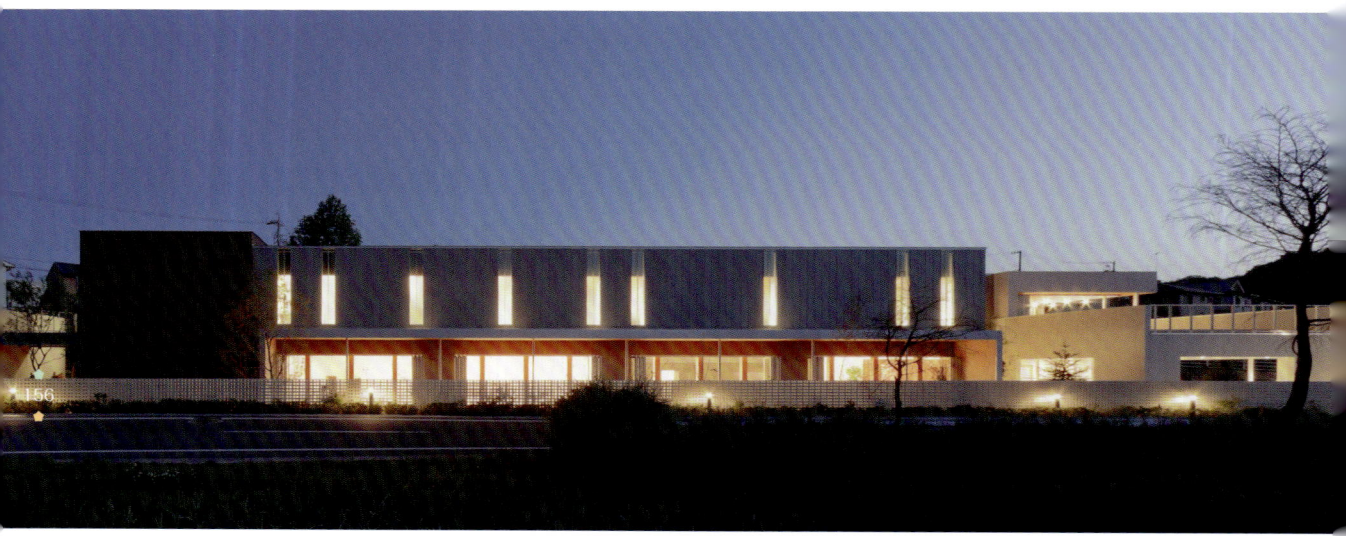

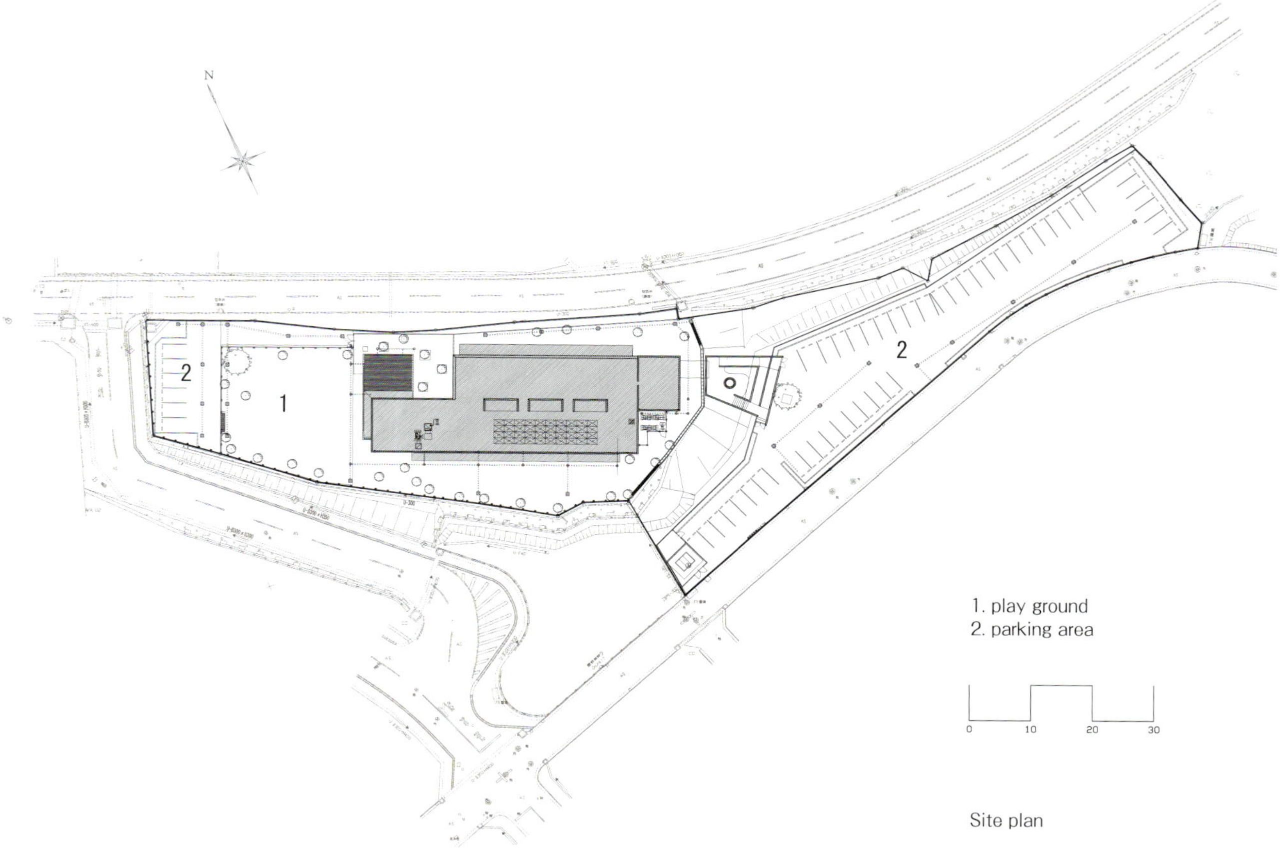
N
1
2
2
1. play ground
2. parking area
0
10
20
30

Site plan

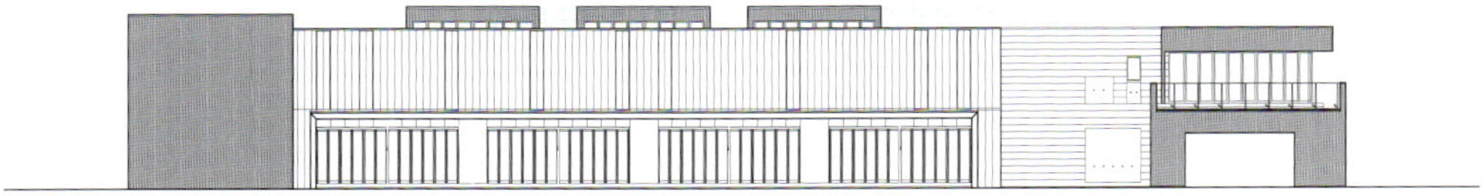

nouth elevation

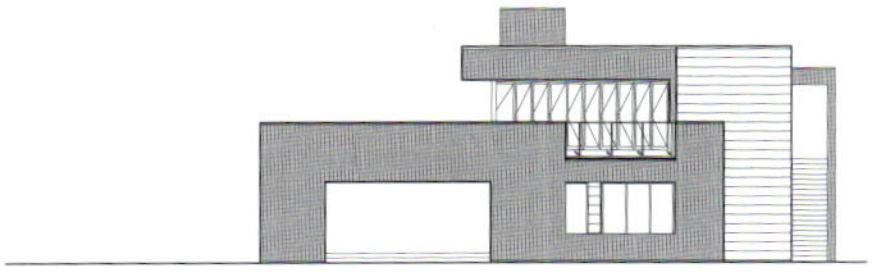

west elevation

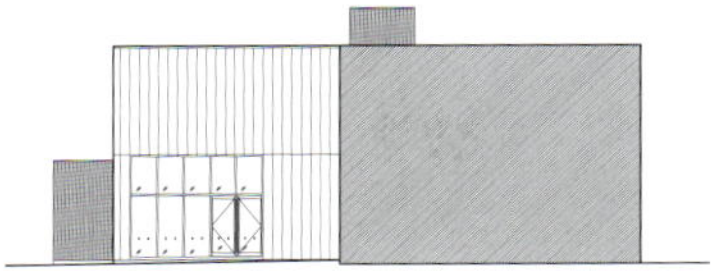

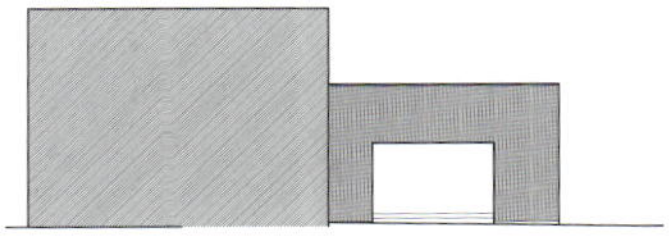

west elevation

east e evation

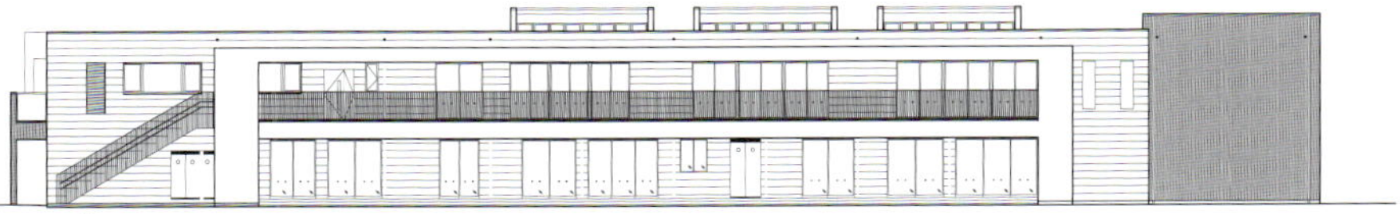

south elevation

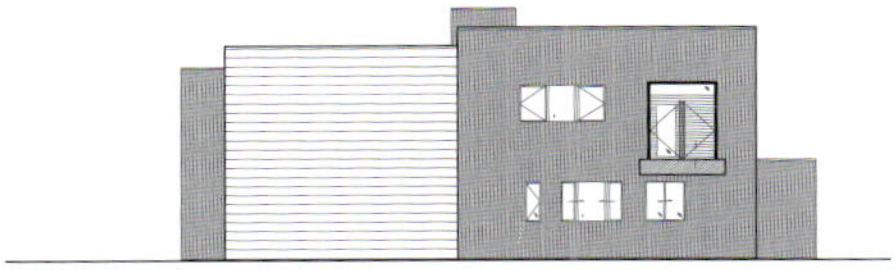

east elevation

TY Nursery

Architects : HIBINOSEKKEI + Youji no Shiro
Country : Japan

TY Nursery

Architects : HIBINOSEKKEI + Youji no Shiro
Country : Japan

TY Nursery

Architects : HIBINOSEKKEI + Youji no Shiro
Country : Japan

TY Nursery

Architects : HIBINOSEKKEI + Youji no Shiro
Country : Japan

TY Nursery

Architects : HIBINOSEKKEI + Youji no Shiro
Country : Japan

166

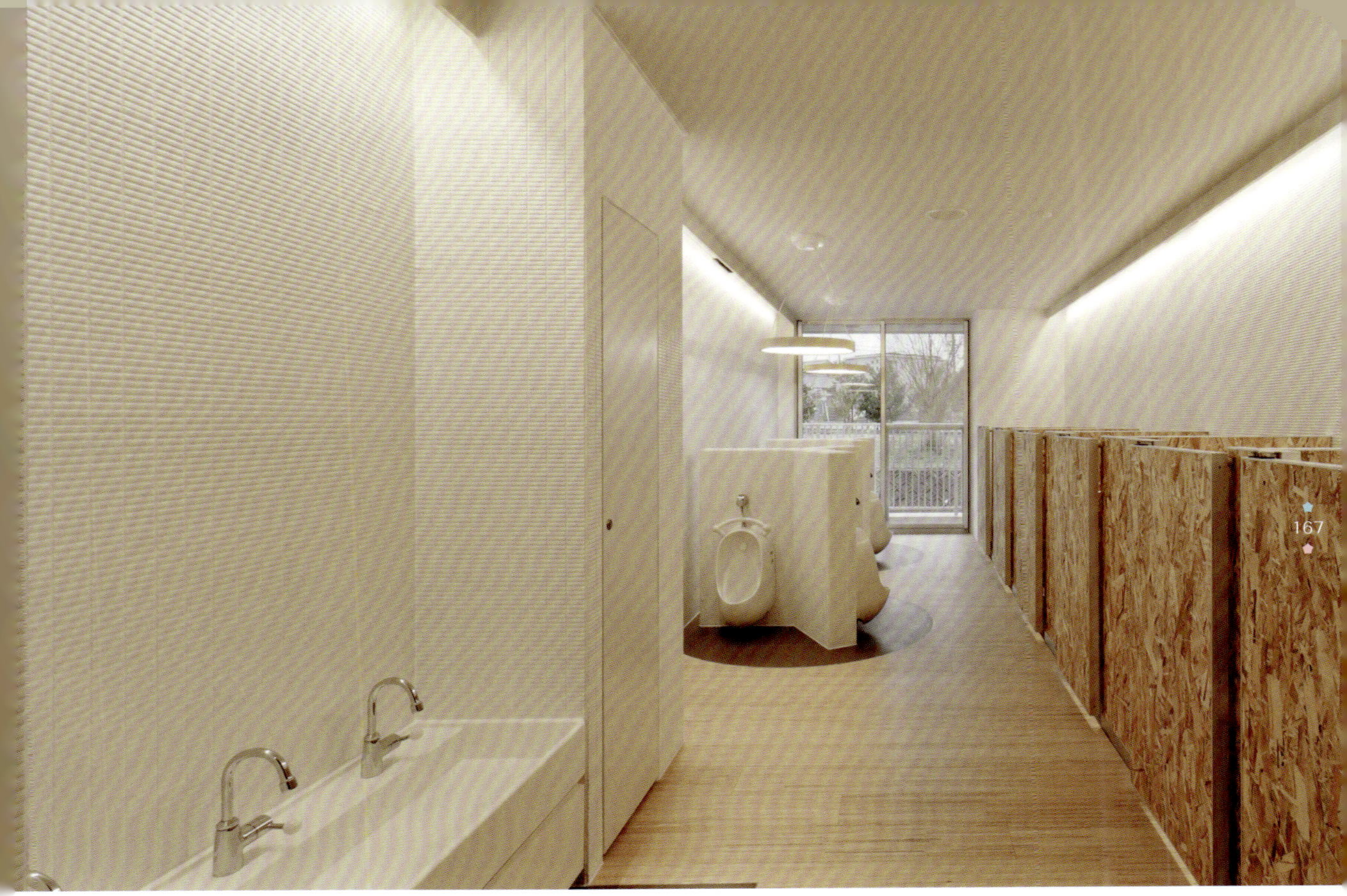

TY Nursery

✿ ✿ ✿

Architects : HIBINOSEKKEI + Youji no Shiro
Country : Japan

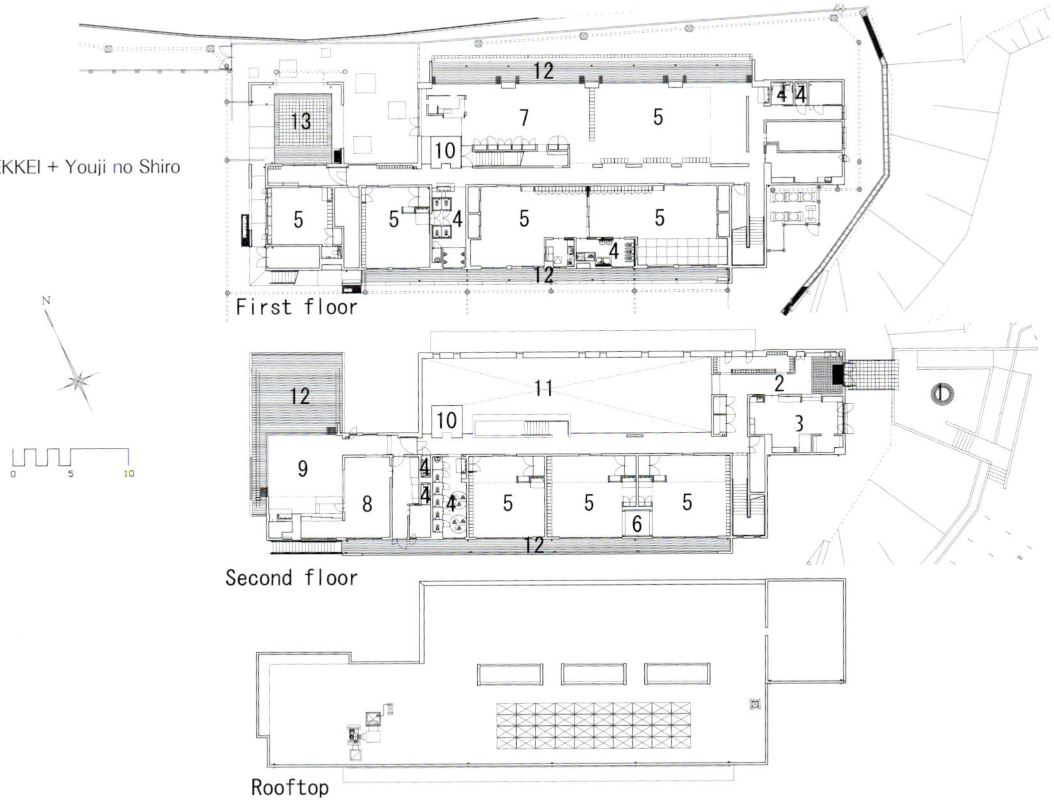

1. approach
2. entrance
3. office
4. restroom
5. childcare room
6. den
7. lounge
8. kitchen
9. dining room
10. EV
11. void
12. play terrace
13. swimming pool

First floor

Second floor

Rooftop

ATM Nursery

This is a nursery at the site which used to be a fire department. It is in a part of Chitose New Town straddling the border between Toyonaka city and Suita city. In this area, communities had been built and developed around the housing estates, but now they are tend to decline and disappear.

Nursery is a place to develop children's personality and also, it's important to tell children the history of their neighborhood and old scenery. Therefore, we reinterpret the housing estates, and plan a nursery as a hub of local communities. For example, the exterior has different kinds of level and give variety in order to avoid the long and thin exterior which is a characteristic of housing estates but gives a ticky-tacky impression. We planned a balcony at the periphery of the building which is also a characteristic of housing estate, where there are undulation, climbing equipment, slope, bench, and a monkey bar. They make children take an exercise playing. In addition, the children's activities are sent out to the neighborhood in the process. Also, in this area, by allowing a light injury and failure, children will built further sense of advancement and challenge.

Making more contacts among people, we planned people's eyes can be spread to any directions. For example, the kitchen and dining room is open to the street or outside of the building. They are also connected to the outside corridor and play terrace so that neighbors can take care of children's activities and for teachers it became easier to notice what is happened outside. In every nursery room, there are large windows at the side of the play terrace and the corridor so that it prompt different ages of children to communicate and feel their presence each other.

Design Agency :
HIBINOSEKKEI + Youji no Shiro (www.e-ensha.com)
Country : Japan
Site area : 2019.70
Surface area : 694.87m²
Building area : 1080.30m²
Photography : Studio Bauhaus, Ryuji Inoue
Project Location : Toyonaka, Osaka, Japan

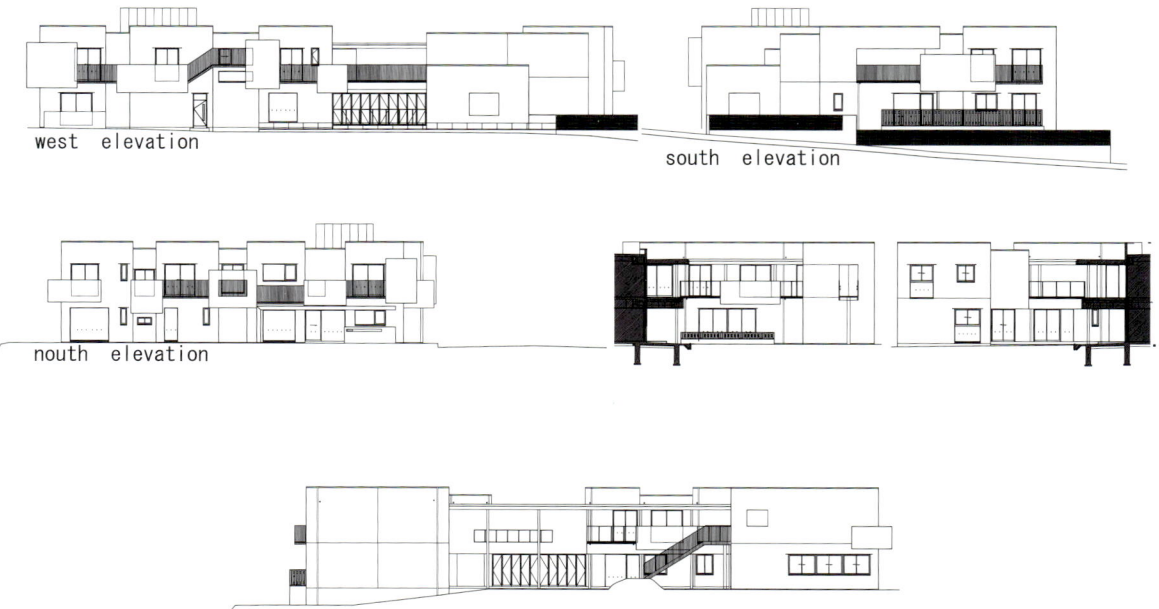

ATM Nursery

* * * *

Architects : HIBINOSEKKEI + Youji no Shiro
Country : Japan

ATM Nursery

Architects : HIBINOSEKKEI + Youji no Shiro
Country : Japan

ATM Nursery

Architects : HIBINOSEKKEI + Youji no Shiro
Country : Japan

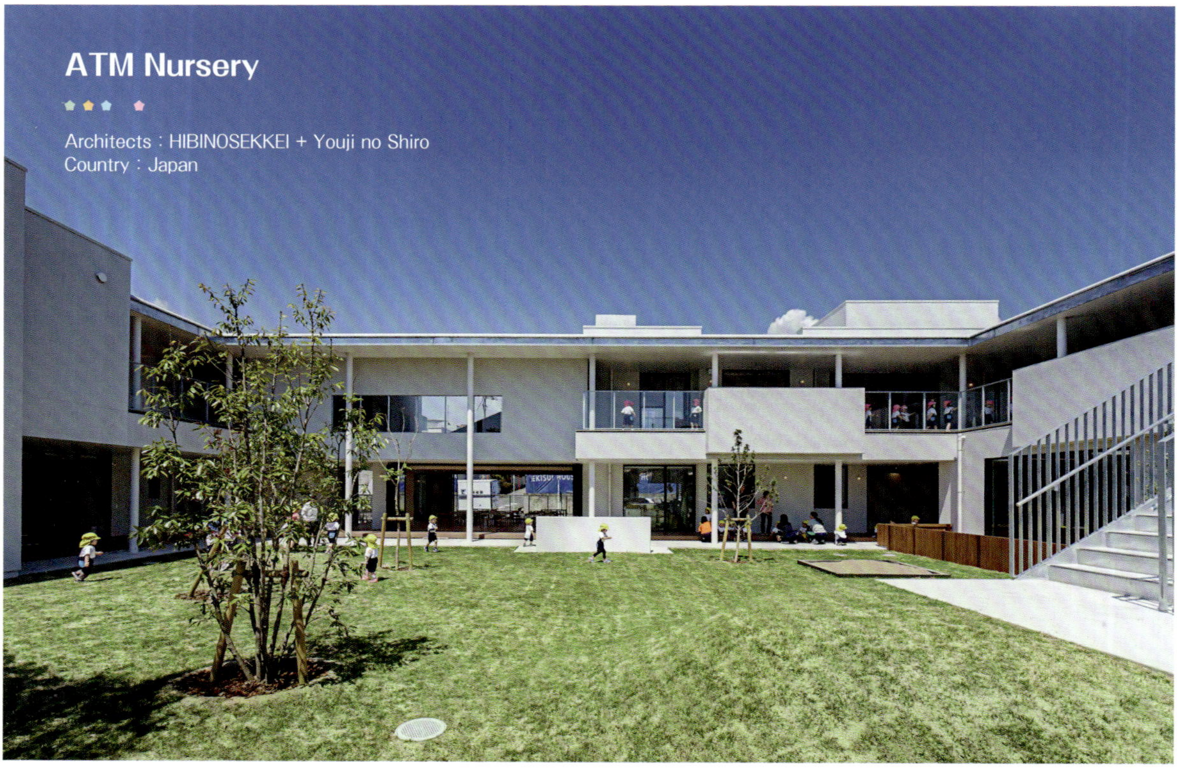

175

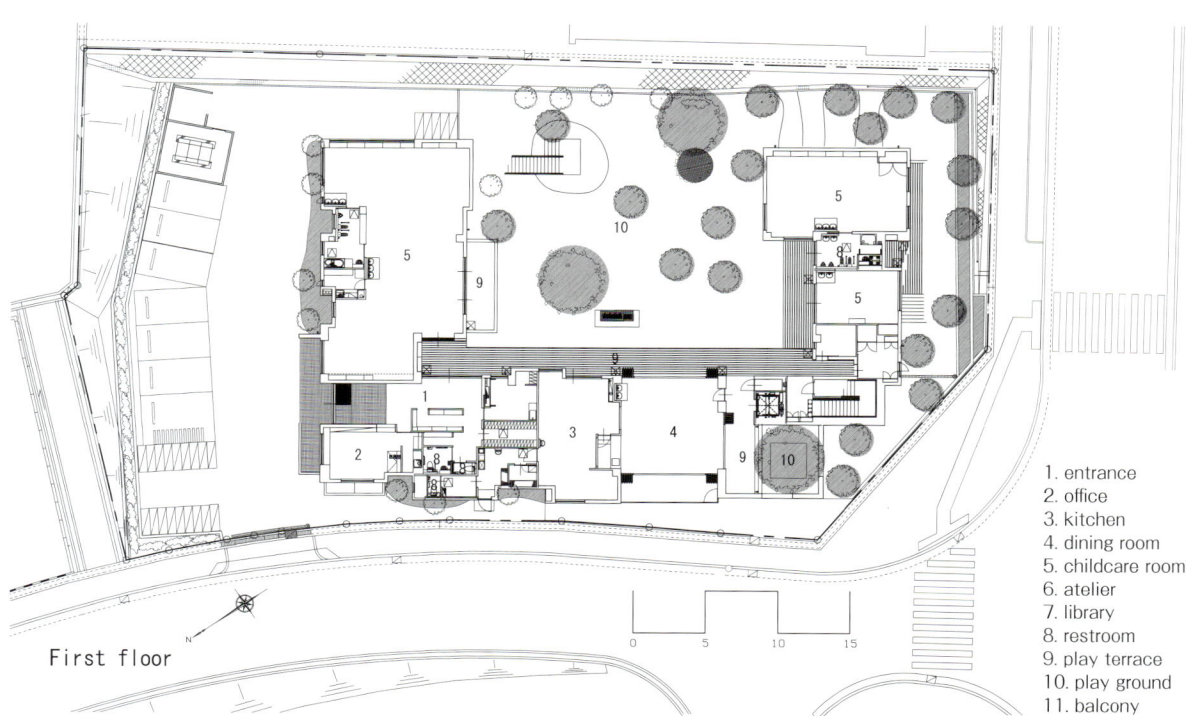

First floor

1. entrance
2. office
3. kitchen
4. dining room
5. childcare room
6. atelier
7. library
8. restroom
9. play terrace
10. play ground
11. balcony

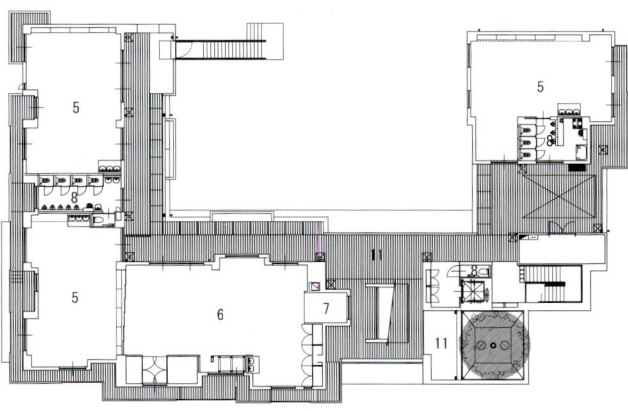

ATM Nursery

Architects : HIBINOSEKKEI + Youji no Shiro
Country : Japan

Second floor

Rooftop

1. entrance
2. office
3. kitchen
4. dining room
5. childcare room
6. atelier
7. library
8. restroom
9. play terrace
10. play ground
11. balcony

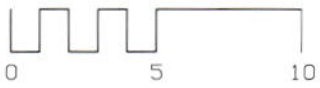

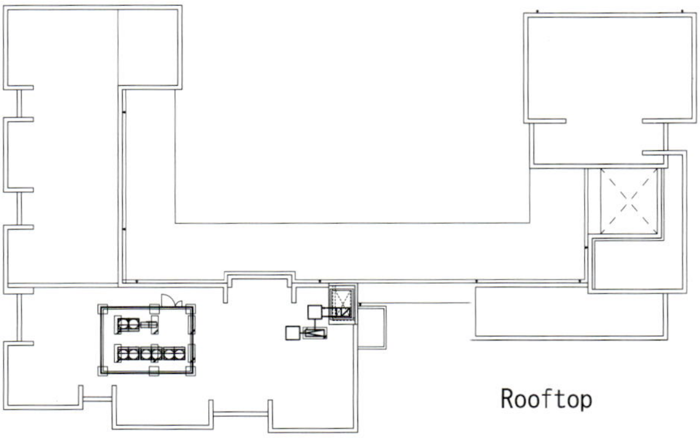

ATM Nursery

* * * *

Architects : HIBINOSEKKEI + Youji no Shiro
Country : Japan

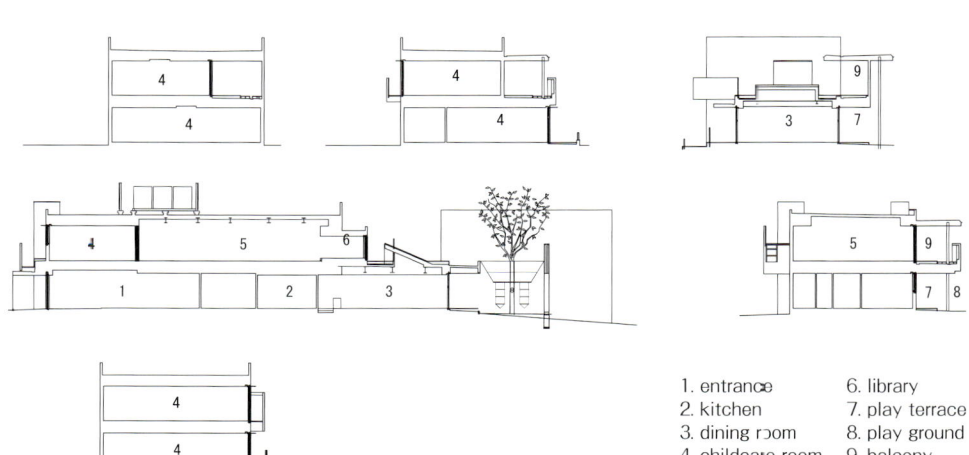

1. entrance
2. kitchen
3. dining room
4. childcare room
5. atelier
6. library
7. play terrace
8. play ground
9. balcony

ATM Nursery

★★★ ★

Architects : HIB NOSEKKEI + Youji no Shiro
Country : Japan

Architects：Takaharu+Yui Tezuka/ Tezuka Architects
Country：Japan
Design Agency：
Tezuka Architects Norihide Imagawa(structure design)/TIS&Partners
Phase I：389.48m²
Phase II：359.48m²
Photography：Tezuka Architects
Client：The Japan Committee for UNICEF
Project Location：Minamisanriku, Motoyoshi, Miyagi, Japan

Asahi Kindergarten

The original Asahi Kindergarten was lost in the Tohoku earthquake on 11 March 2011. Tezuka Architects, funded by Japan Committee for UNICEF, designed and reconstructed the Asahi Kindergarten on a highland area by using the huge trees that killed by the salt water of 2011 tsunami. These trees have meaningful symbols for the local villagers as they were planted along the approach to Daioji Temple, the main temple on the hill which its height is just enough to elude tsunamis in the long history. Many villagers survived because the priest of the temple used to teach them to escape to the temple.

The aim for the project was to express that the tree was not only the building materials used to construct the school but it is where it is home to the spirit of the town people. Reusing the killed trees to create a new kindergarten for the next generation of the town reaffirms hope held by everyone in Tohoku or Japan.

Every piece of the building including structure, floor and handrail, was curved out from these trees which planted after tsunami in 1611, exactly 400 years before the tsunami in 2011. Traditional joinery and wedges without any metal joints were used, because these old techniques have made Japanese traditional architecture survive more than 1300 years. There is a massive column with sectional dimension of 600mm x 600mm erected on the building as how it originally stood on the ground. The project bears a message for those children who will likely encounter a tsunami in the next 400 years.

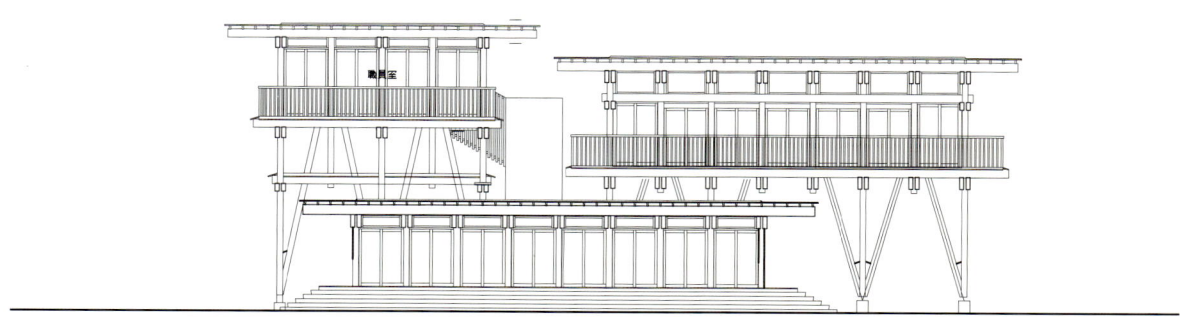

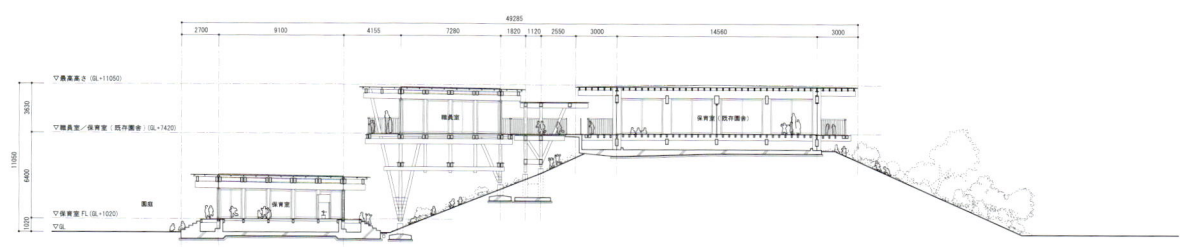

Asahi Kindergarten

Architects : Takaharu+Yui Tezuka/ Tezuka Architects
Country : Japan

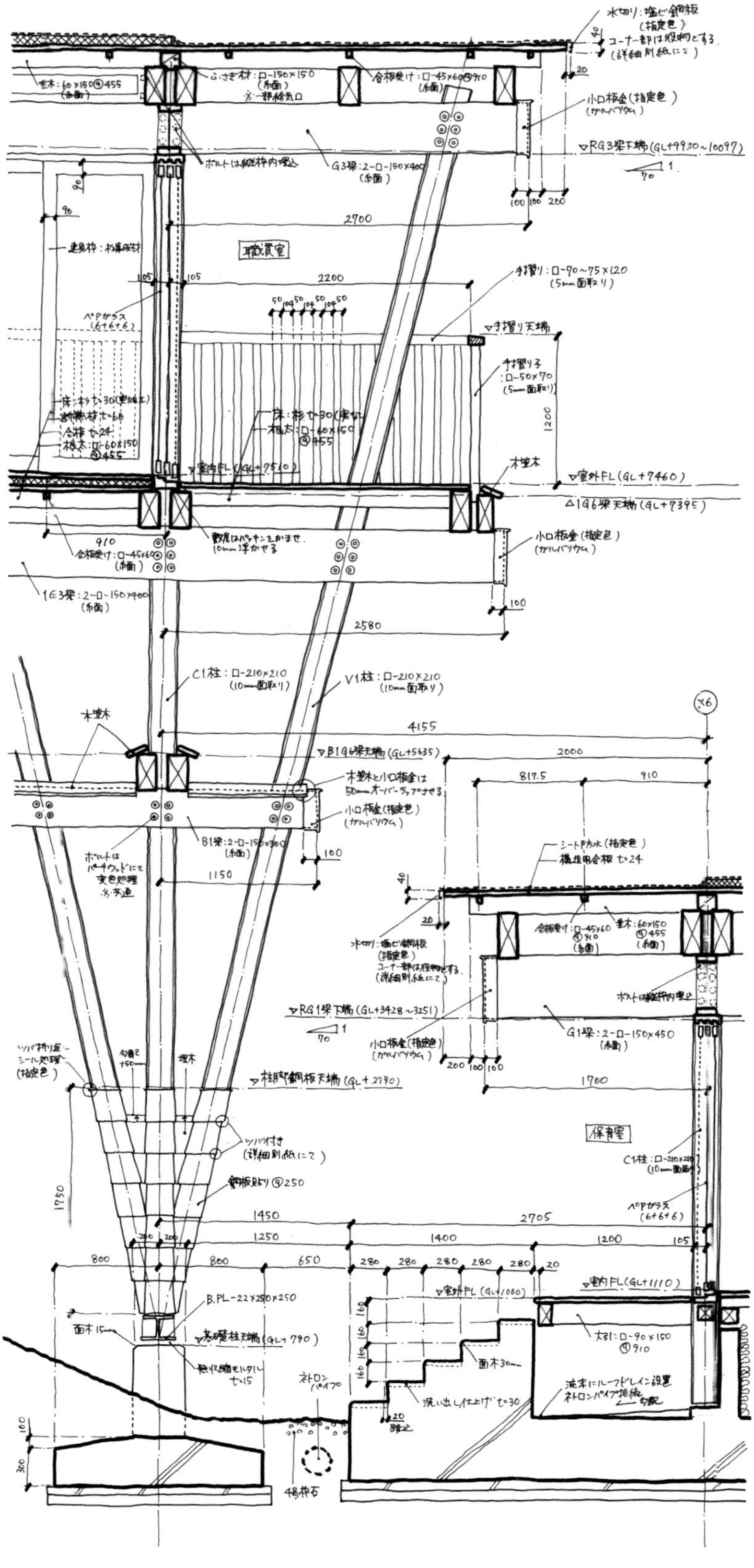

水切り：塩ビ鋼板
(指定色)
コーナー部は役物とする
(詳細別紙にて)
垂木：60×150 @455
(両面)
ふさぎ材：□-150×150
(両面)
※一部換気口
合板受け：□-45×60 @910
(両面)
小口板金(指定色)
(ガルバリウム)
ボルトは縦枠内埋込
G3梁：2-□-150×400
(両面)
▽RG3梁下端(GL+9930~10097)
100 100 200
2700
建具枠：杉集成材
職員室
2200
105
ペアガラス
(6+6+6)
手摺り：□-70~75×120
(5mm面取り)
▽手摺り天端
手摺り子
□-50×70
(5mm面取り)
1200
床：杉 t=30(実加工)
断熱材 t=60
合板 t=24
根太：□-60×150
@455
床：杉 t=30(実加工)
根太：□-60×150
@455
▽室内FL(GL+7510)
木笠木
▽室外FL(GL+7460)
△1G6梁天端(GL+7395)
910
合板受け：□-45×60
(両面)
敷居はパッキンをかませ、10mm浮かせる
小口板金(指定色)
(ガルバリウム)
1E3梁：2-□-150×400
(両面)
100
2580
C1柱：□-210×210
(10mm面取り)
V1柱：□-210×210
(10mm面取り)
X6
木笠木
4155
▽B1G6梁天端(GL+5635)
2000
木笠木と小口板金は50mmオーバーラップさせる
817.5
910
小口板金(指定色)
(ガルバリウム)
B1梁：2-□-150×300
(両面)
100
ボルトはパテ・ウッドにて変色処理
※共通
1150
シート防水(指定色)
構造用合板 t=24
合板受け：□-45×60 @910
(両面)
垂木：60×150
@455
(両面)
水切り：塩ビ鋼板
(指定色)
コーナー部は役物とする
(詳細別紙にて)
ボルトは縦枠内埋込
▽RG1梁下端(GL+3428~3251)
G1梁：2-□-150×450
(両面)
小口板金(指定色)
(ガルバリウム)
200 100 100
1700
ツバ折り返し
シール処理
(指定色)
勾配
埋木
▽柱脚部鋼板天端(GL+2790)
保育室
ツバ付き
(詳細別紙にて)
C1柱：□-210×210
(10mm面取り)
鋼板貼り @250
ペアガラス
(6+6+6)
1750
1450
2705
1250
1400
1200
105
800
800
650
280 280 280 280 280
20
▽室内FL(GL+1110)
▽室外FL(GL+1060)
B.PL-22×250×250
面木15
▽基礎柱天端(GL+790)
無収縮モルタル t=15
面木30
大引：□-90×150
@910
流末にルーフドレイン設置
ネトロンパイプ接続
ネトロンパイプ
洗い出し仕上げ t=30
4号砕石
100
300

Asahi Kindergarten

Architects : Takaharu+Yui Tezuka/ Tezuka Architects
Country : Japan

Asahi Kindergarten

Architects : Takaharu+Yui Tezuka/ Tezuka Architects
Country : Japan

189

HF & VUC Fyn

Located next to the central station the HF & VUC Fyn complex marks an important step towards the realisation of a new city campus that ties the inner city and the harbour together. By combining elements from its coarse industrial neighbours with an embracing and transparent interior organisation the HF & VUC Fyn aims at bridging between the scale of the harbour and urban life. The building's robust and unassuming exterior is contrasted by an inner spatial diversity of rounded forms that create a varied learning environment for 1.300 students – an inspiring and vivid school that continuously suggests new ways of use and makes room for individual learning needs in a collective building.

The building is characterized by a system of curved lines and rounded forms, which cut through the rational volume's regular form and create a multifaceted spatial setting that takes into account the school's different functions: an arena for teaching and learning, a workplace and a social meeting place for a diverse group of users. The building is organized around a transparent and very active atrium space, called the Agora and named after the public gathering place in ancient Greek cities that constituted the centre of political, spiritual and artistic life in the city state. This central space not only functions as a forum for social activities, but also as an essential learning environment in connection and interplay with the class rooms and the school's additional functions. The rounded shapes form a series of balconies and platforms with shifting overlaps across the atrium in order to create single, double and triple

Design Agency : CEBRA
Country : Denmark
Partners : Mikkel Frost, Carsten Primdahl,
Kolja Nielsen and Mikkel Ha lundbæk Schlesinger
Photographer : Mikkel Frost / CEBRA
Dimensions : 12,500m² new building,
1,100 m² parking basement
Project Location : Odense, Denmark

HF & VUC Fyn

* * * *

Design Agency : CEBRA
Country : Denmark

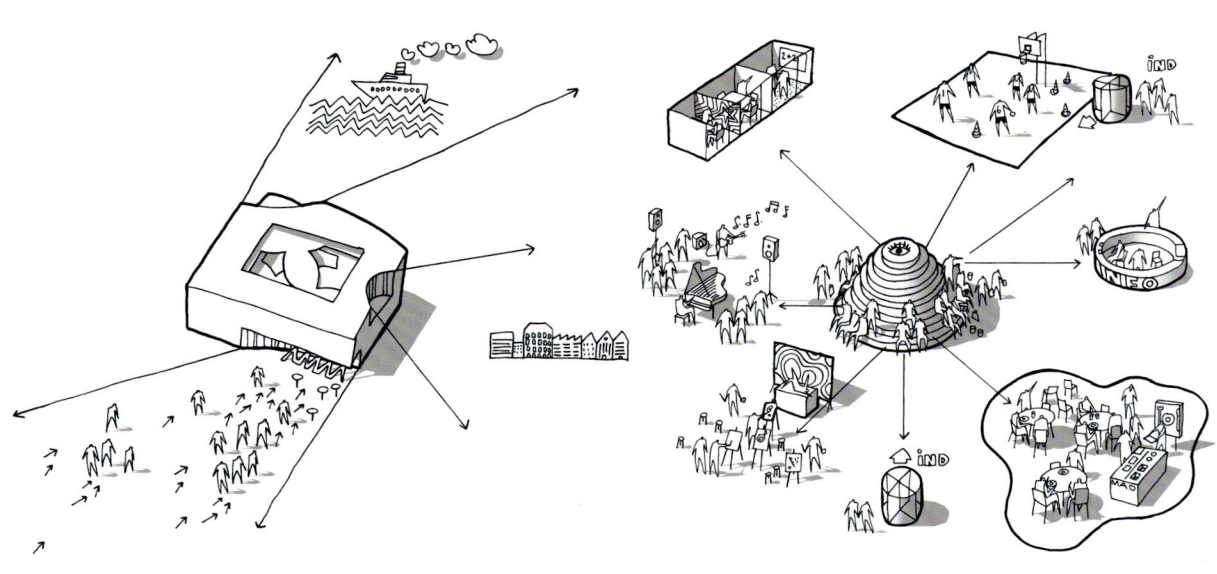

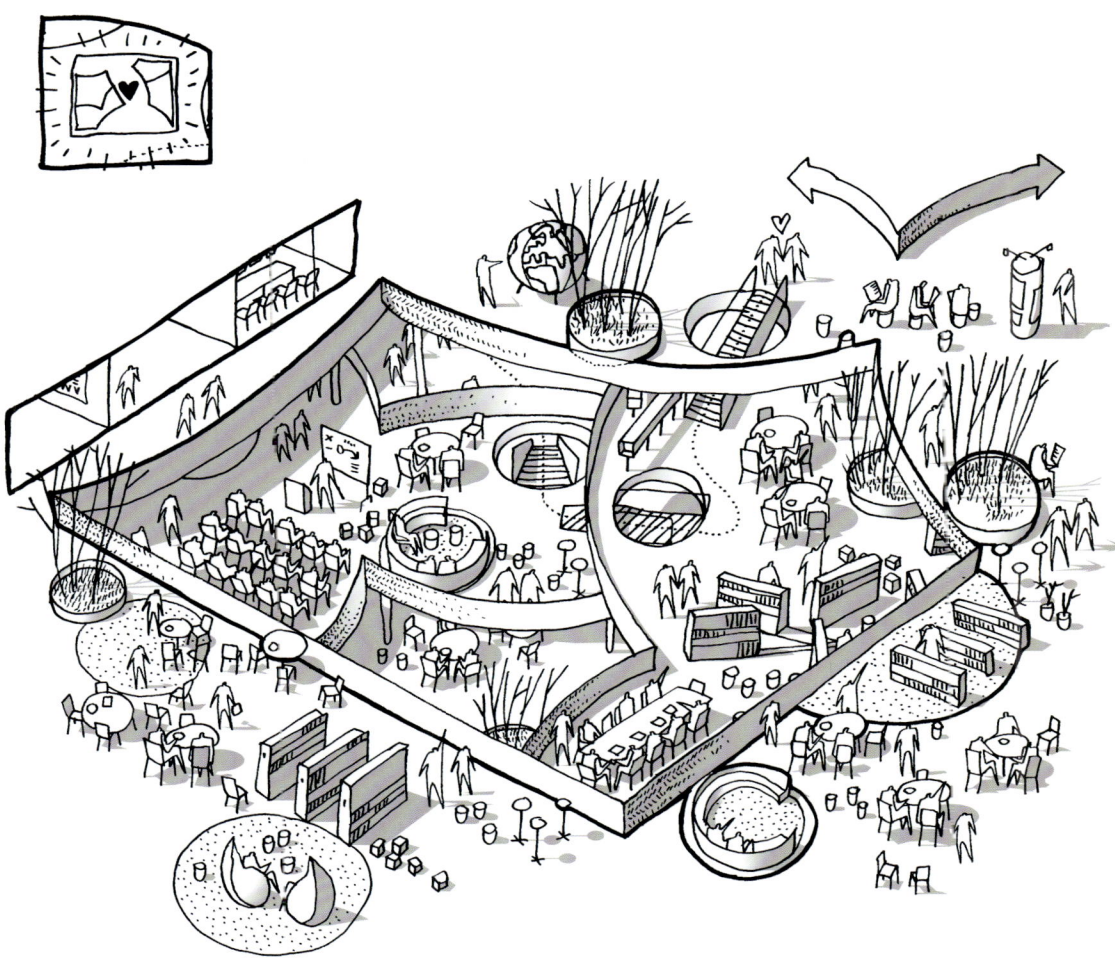

HF & VUC Fyn

Design Agency : CEBRA
Country : Denmark

HF & VUC Fyn

Design Agency : CEBRA
Country : Denmark

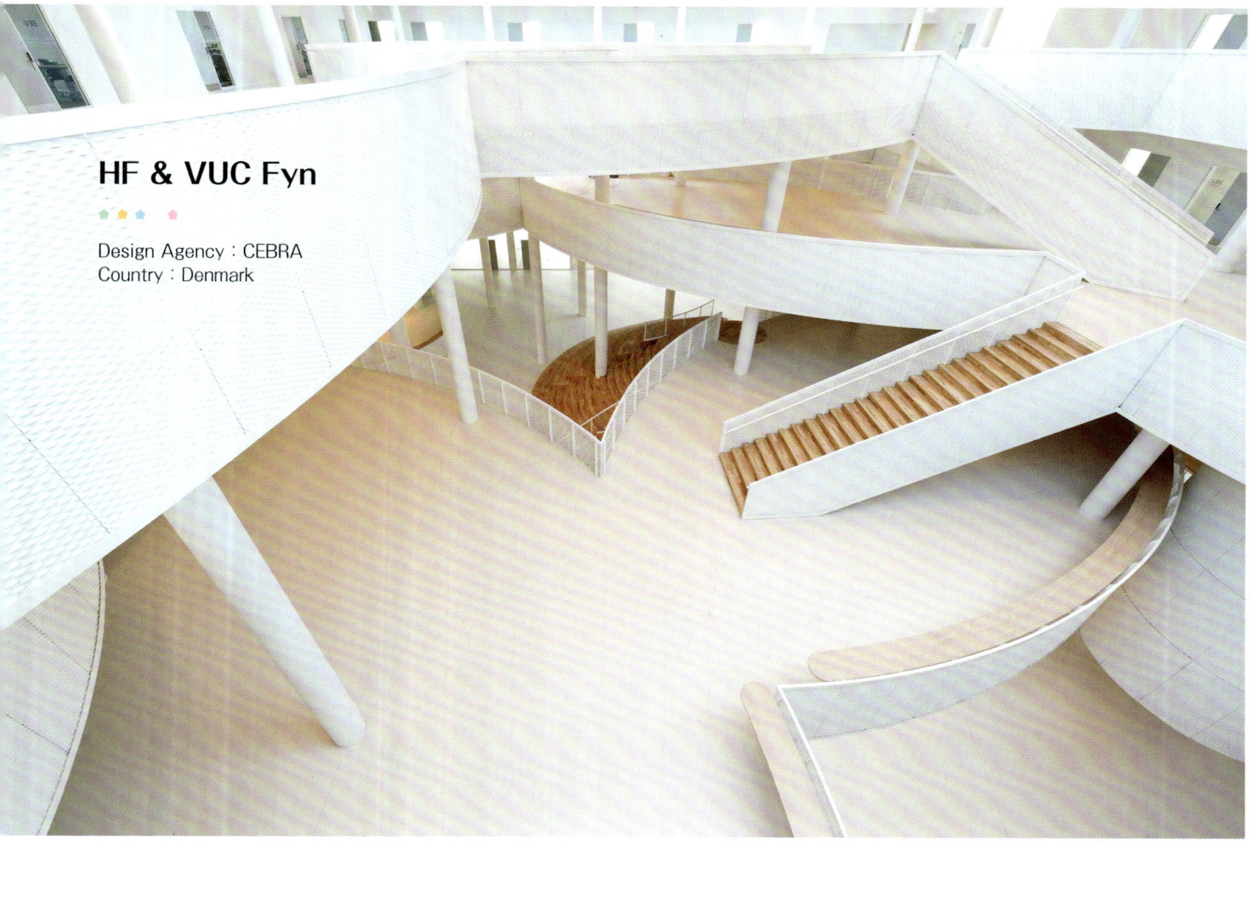

HF & VUC Fyn

Design Agency : CEBRA
Country : Denmark

199

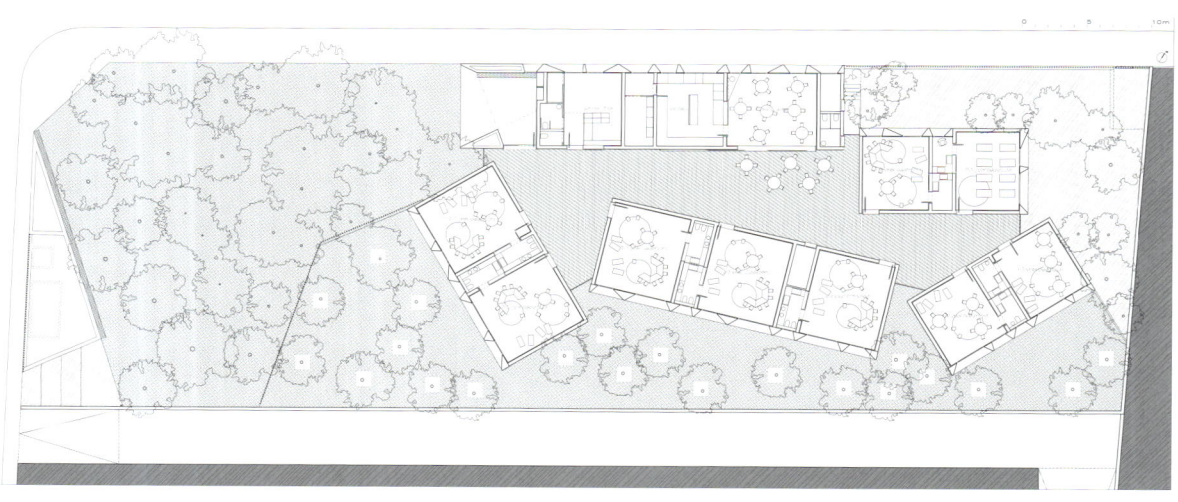

Architects : Aballosllopis architects/ F-VA studio
Country : Spain
Architect director : Enrique Fernández-Vivancos/ Ana Ábalos/ Pablo Llopis
Photographer : José Manuel Cutillas
Client : Benicàssim town council
Project Location : Benicàssim, Spain

CAN FELIÇ NURSERY

The design of Can Felic offers us the opportunity to investigate the concepts of the one and the multiple, the same and the different, as a way to deepen the understanding of the human relationships that are established between the individual and society.

Given that a nursery education program is being developed for children aged 0-3, the objective of this project is not only to fit out and equip the necessary space for learning, but also to ensure that a tranquil and protected atmosphere is created, suitable for both recreation and teaching. The composition cell is defined as the unit made up of two rooms grouped around an area made up of service and communal installations, optimizing the running of the nursery. These cells are located around a central space, a covered plaza, surrounded by separate small pavilions that open onto an exterior patio, that combine to form a play area that complements the patio.

The fan-like orientation of the pavilions around the covered plaza is a liberation from the strict logic of parcelling out, and seeks a link with the passing of the sun from east to west, the presence of trees and the oblique view to the patios to achieve the largest possible focal depth in the available space.

Each group of eight children form a small family and to each one is assigned an independent place, a home. All are equal and at the same time are different according to their position relative to the sun, the view and the relationship with their neighbors. Together they form a community that gathers around the central space has continuity in a grove of trees where the units are sheltered, a courtyards house in the woods. The grove grows and merges with the urban space forming a publicly accessible garden overlooking the Desierto de las Palmas, the fundamental landscape of the common identity of Benicàssim. Can Felic - a courtyard house in the forest in the countryside of Benicàssim.

CAN FELIÇ NURSERY

• • • •

Architects : Abalosllopis architects/ F-VA studio
Country : Spain

CAN FELIÇ NURSERY

Architects : Abalosllopis architects/ F-VA studio
Country : Spain

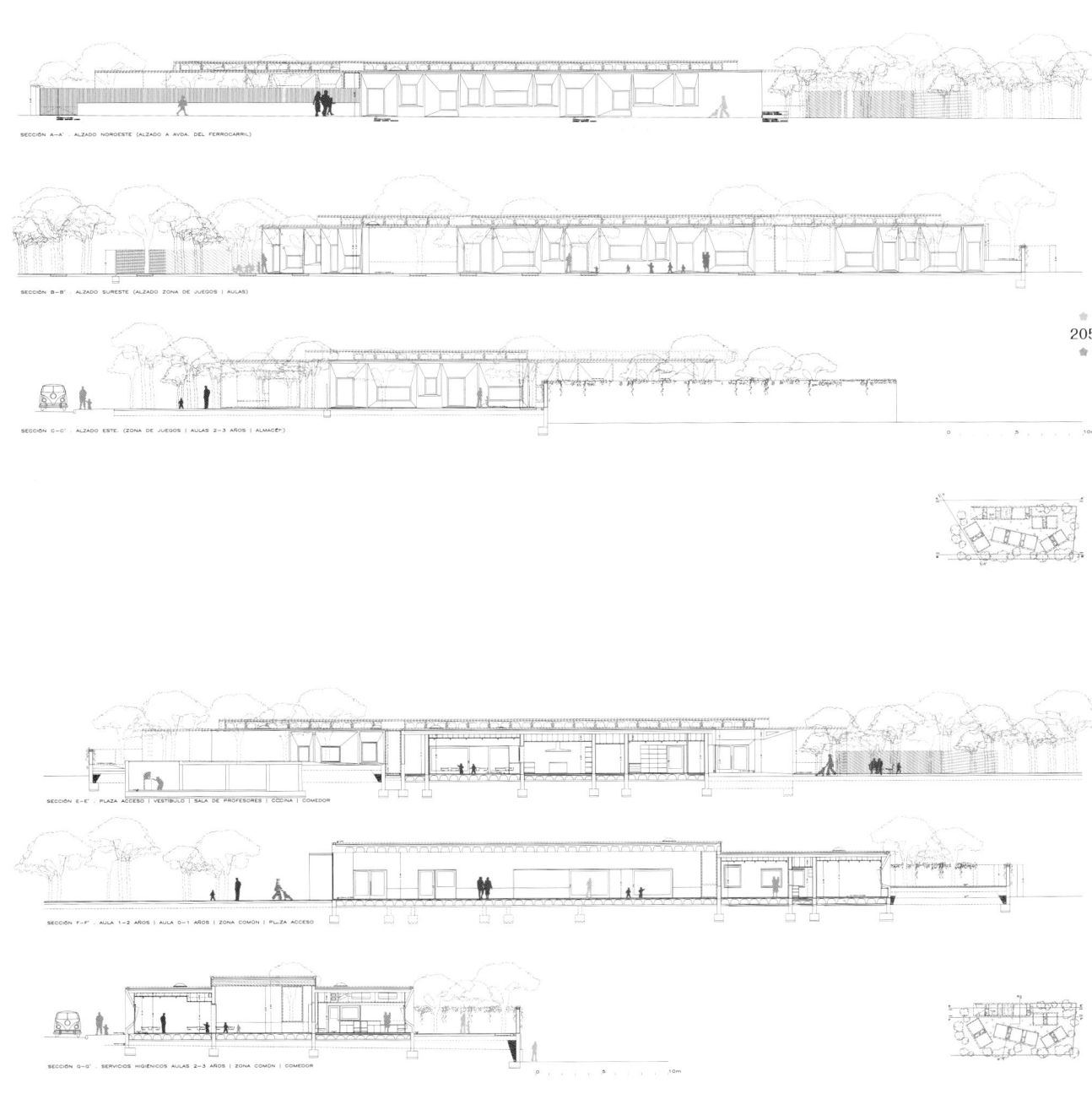

CAN FELIÇ NURSERY

Architects : Abalosllopis architects/ F-VA studio
Country : Spain

CAN FELIÇ NURSERY

Architects : Abalosllopis architects/ F-VA studio
Country : Spain

CAN FELIÇ NURSERY

Architects : Abalosllopis architects/ F-VA studio
Country : Spain

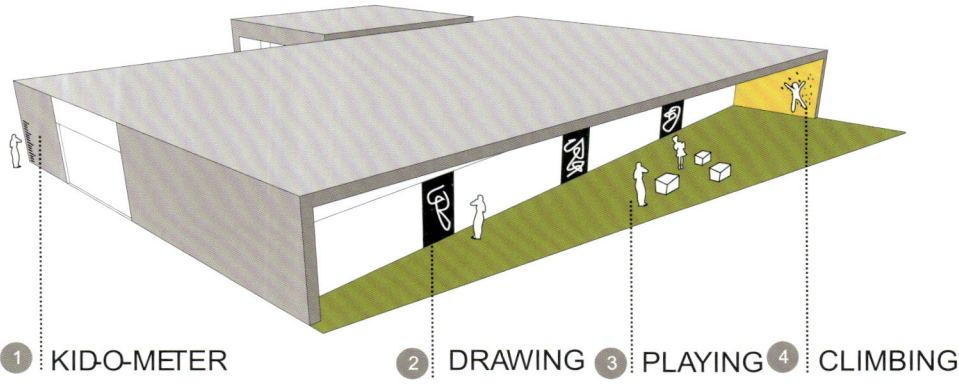

1. KID-O-METER 2. DRAWING 3. PLAYING 4. CLIMBING

Design Agency : Arhitektura Jure Kotnik
Country : Slovenia
Creative Director : Jure Kotnik
Photographer : Janez Marolt
Dimensions : 696m²
Client : MO Slovenj Gradec
Project Location : Podgorje, Slovenj Gradec

Open kindergarten Podgorje

New Time Share Kindergarten is located in the central area of small Slovenian village settlement Podgorje. The building is an extension of an existing school and hosts four playrooms and a classroom for first graders. The kindergarten's special feature is its open plan approach with unified play space, which covers as much as 86% of the entire kindergarten and can be closed off if necessary. Children can move inside the kindergarten without restrictions, according to the so-called timeshare principle. Movement is even encouraged by a series of elements like sliding doors between playrooms, accordion doors of the central common room, and the road meandering between playrooms, which visually connects different spaces and invites children to follow it (walk, run, ride their kick scooter or bike). Even special road signs have been designed, encouraging children to mimic movements of a particular animal (butterfly, crab, lizard, etc.), and go either fast (cheetah) or slow (snail).

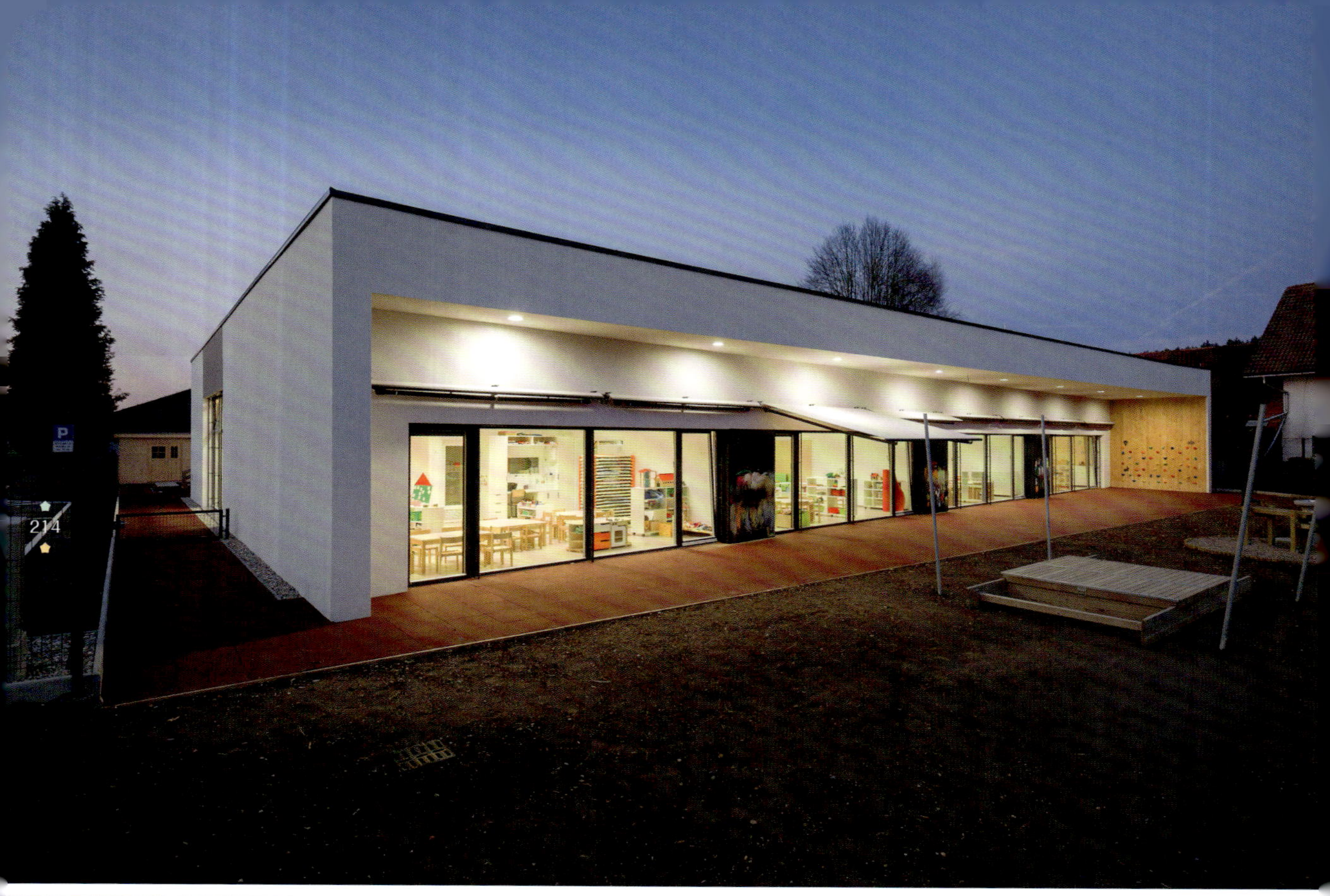

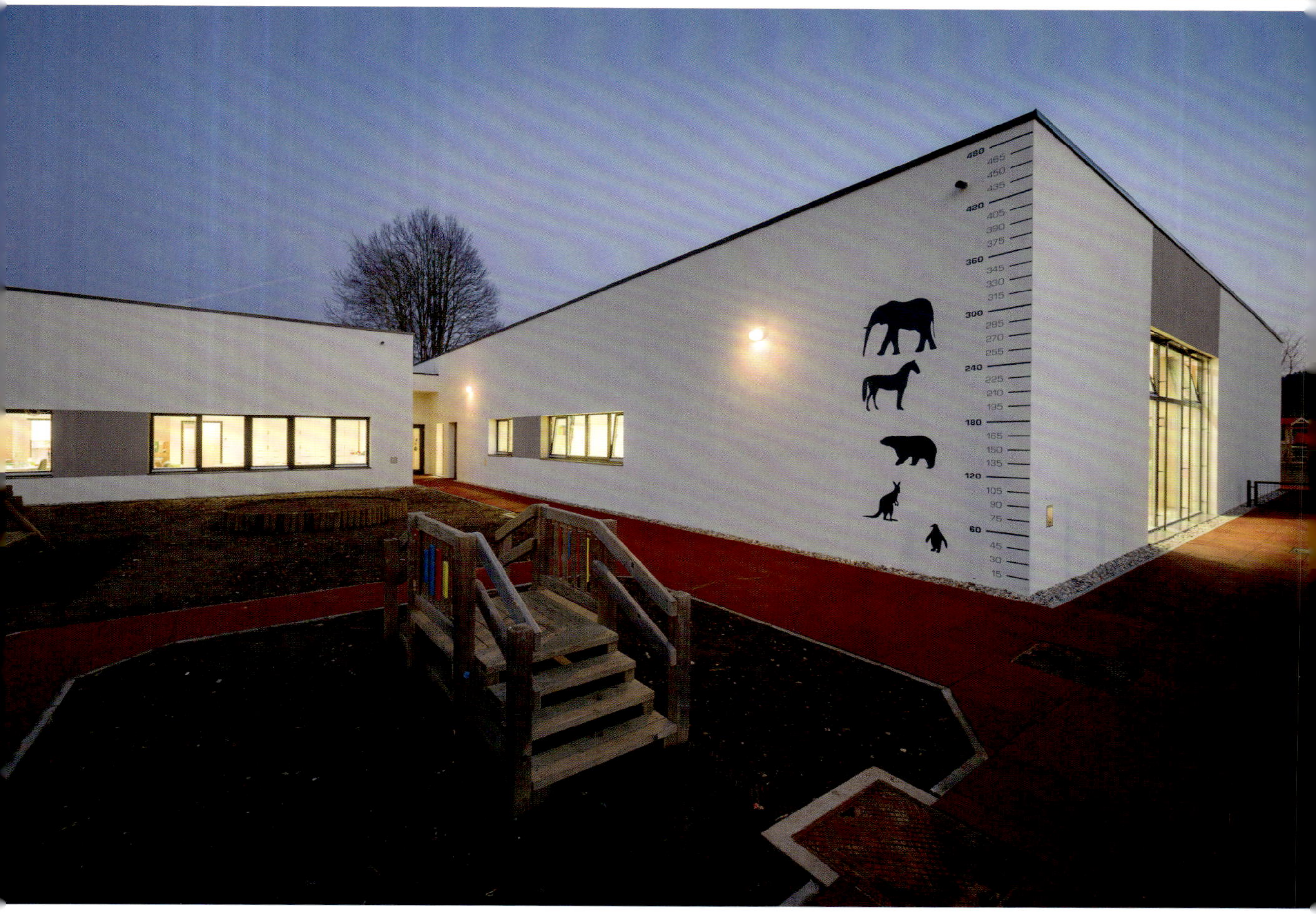
480
465
450
435
420
405
390
375
360
345
330
315
300
285
270
255
240
225
210
195
180
165
150
135
120
105
90
75
60
45
30
15

Open kindergarten Podgorje

Design Agency : Arhitektura Jure Kotnik
Country : Slovenia

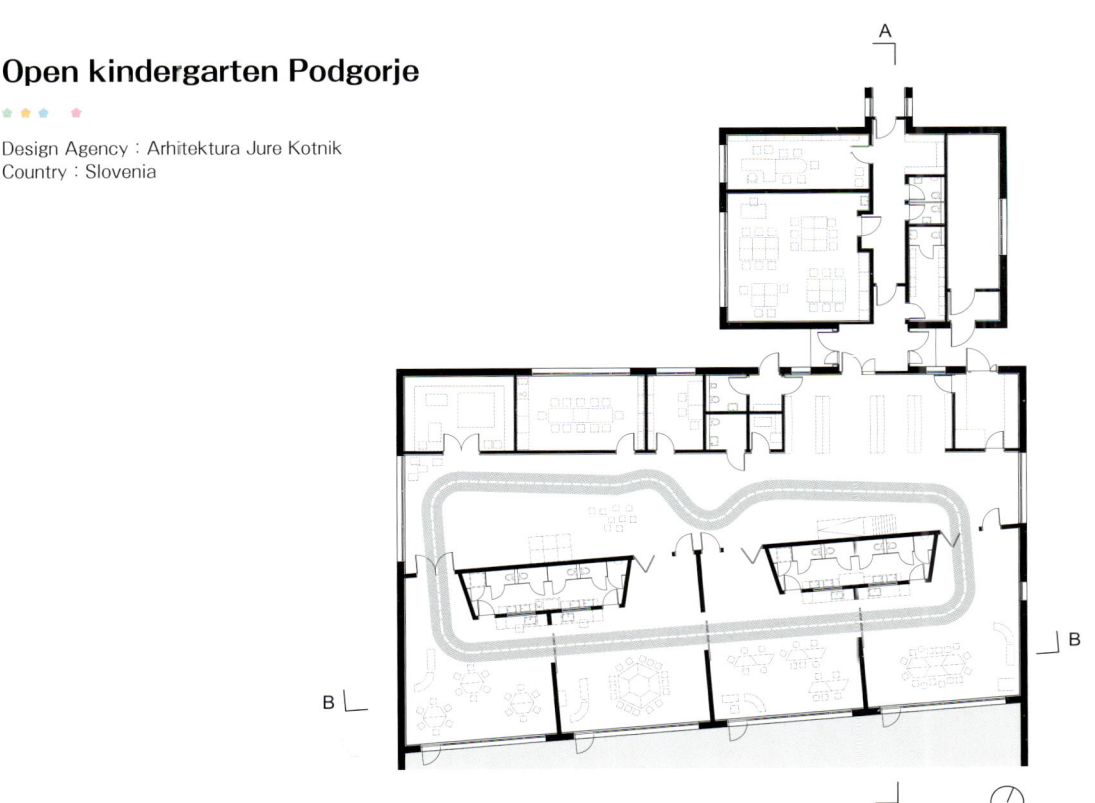

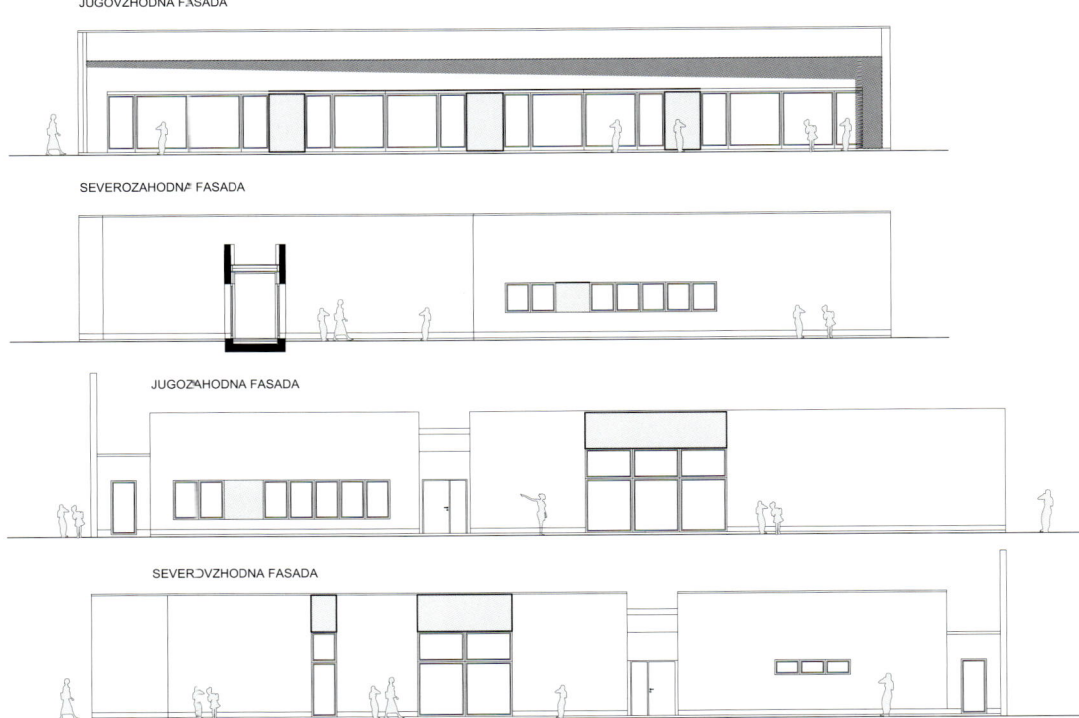

Open kindergarten Podgorje

Design Agency : Arhitektura Jure Kotnik
Country : Slovenia

Open kindergarten Podgorje

Design Agency : Arhitektura Jure Kotnik
Country : Slovenia

220

Open kindergarten Podgorje

Design Agency : Arhitektura Jure Kotnik
Country : Slovenia

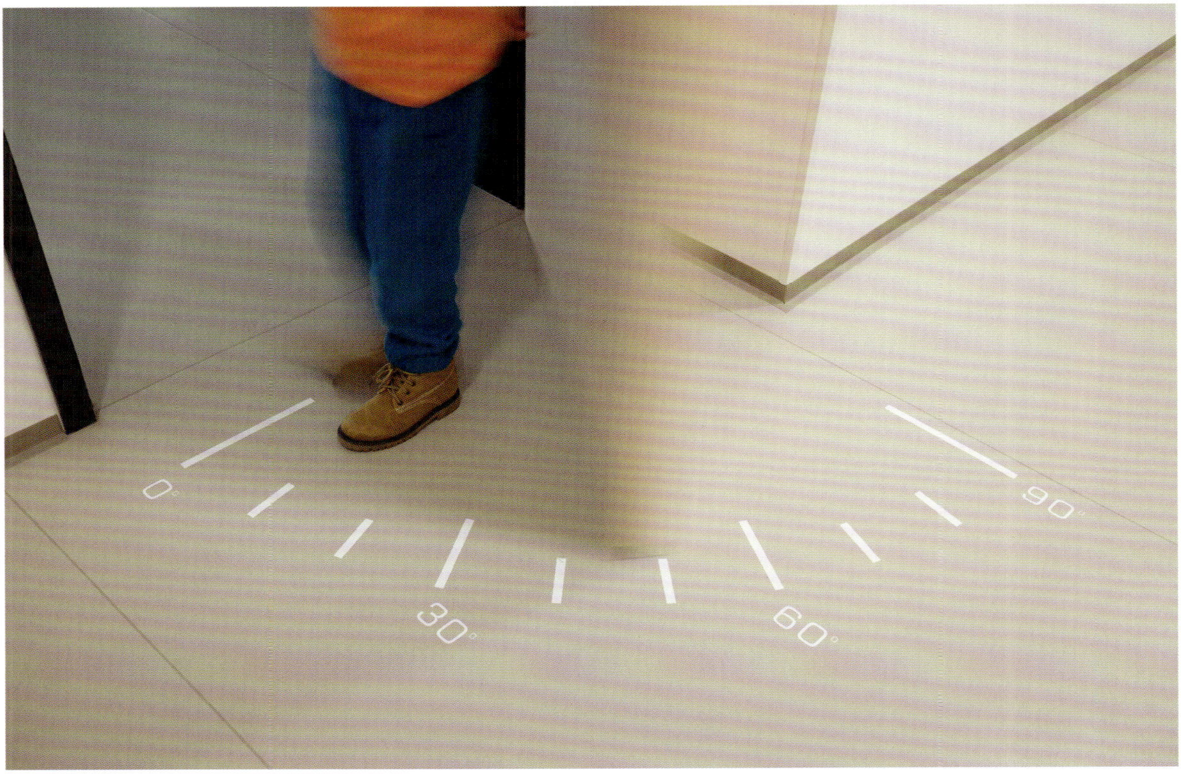

Open kindergarten Podgorje

Design Agency : Arhitektura Jure Kotnik
Country : Slovenia

Open Sport Kindergarten Minsk

Children today lack of physical activities and Timeshare sport kindergarten is designed to address this issue. The design focus is to encourage movement and physical activity, which has proven to have a positive effect on the development of children's body and mind. Physical activity helps improving also their concentration and ability to memorize, while at the same time they develop their social skills through sport. Sport orientation of the kindergarten can be seen on all levels of the building. On the outside, there are two hockey goals as a part of the wooden, while on the inside there is abundance of sport equipment and two sport halls for hundred. One hall is for practice ballet, the other for group sports and climbing, lots of equipment is mobile and can be moved around the building. Even parts of the furniture are designed to support sport as fro example desk for teachers than can also be used as indoor football goal. Several other elements have double use as well, as stairs that form an amphitheater with colorful cushions or cupboard doors in the playrooms that are used as blackboards for drawing. In the ballet hall there is a special smaller modular amphitheater that can be quickly turned into tables and chairs that can transform the place quickly into additional playroom or space for other activities. Playrooms are designed to be spacious and open, with fully glassed wall orientated towards the playground. Between the playrooms there are sliding doors that ease cooperation and exchange among kids of different groups and ages. Playroom floors have several special floor signs that indicate different sport activities as basketball, football or hopscotch and even a road that goes through two playrooms and central space. Kids can ride their scooters along the way and with special children traffic signs they may also learn the basics of traffic.

The exterior of the kindergarten offers a series of spaces for different sports and play activities. Special innovation is an elliptical football field - the shape of the ellipse reflects better the movement of the children while the deviation from the established or expected form of the playground unconsciously encourages mental creativity. Beside the tradition play equipment there is also an athletics area and multi-purpose platform that can be used for several sport activities. Each playroom has its own wooden playground pavilion, which protects children against strong summer sun or the rain in case of bad weather. In the middle of the playground there is also a small hill for sledding, skiing, rope climbing and other motor activities, while the rest of the free surfaces can be used to organize various sport polygons or in winter very popular cross-country skiing.

Design Agency : Arhitektura Jure Kotnik
Country : Slovenia
Creative Director : Jure Kotnik
Photographer : Riko d.d.
Dimensions : 696m²
Client : Riko d.d and City of Minsk
Project Location : Minsk, Belarus

Open Sport Kindergarten Minsk

Design Agency : Arhitektura Jure Kotnik
Country : Slovenia

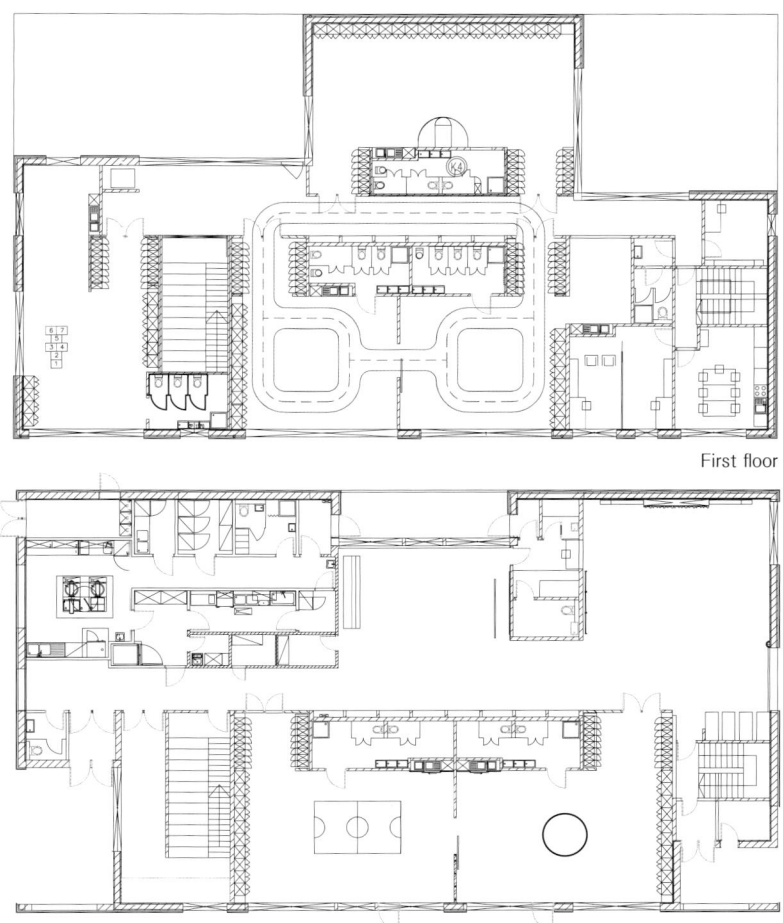

First floor

Ground floor

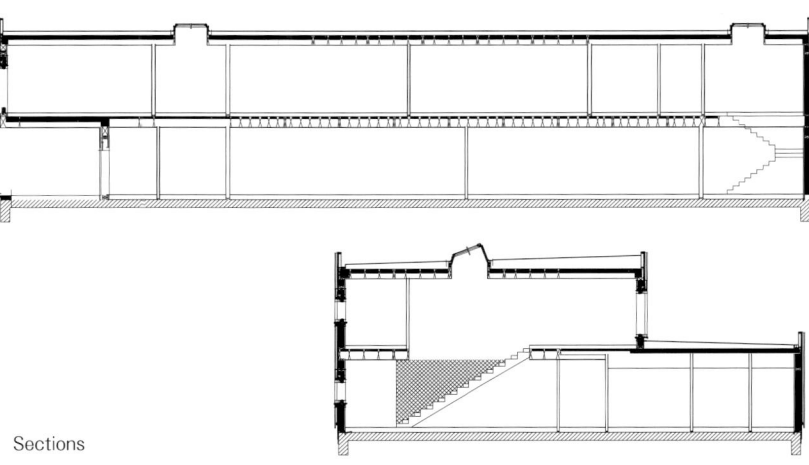

Sections

Open Sport Kindergarten Minsk

Design Agency : Arhitektura Jure Kotnik
Country : Slovenia

230

Open Sport Kindergarten Minsk

Design Agency : Arhitektura Jure Kotnik
Country : Slovenia

232

Open Sport Kindergarten Minsk

Design Agency : Arhitektura Jure Kotnik
Country : Slovenia

Open Sport Kindergarten Minsk

Design Agency : Arhitektura Jure Kotnik
Country : Slovenia

Open Sport Kindergarten Minsk

Design Agency : Arhitektura Jure Kotnik
Country : Slovenia

Open Sport Kindergarten Minsk

Design Agency : Arhitektura Jure Kotnik
Country : Slovenia

Design Agency : Arhitektura Jure Kotnik
Country : Slovenia
Creative Director : Jure Kotnik
Photographer : Janez Marolt
Dimensions : 1040m²
Client : MO Slovenj Gradec
Project Location : Šmartno, Slovenj Gradec

Open Timeshare Kindergarten Šmartno

Open Timeshare Kindergarten in Šmartno was designed to encourage interaction, peer learning and self-learning. It has an open floor plan, which merges poorly used spaces such as wardrobes, corridors and stairs into one learning landscape together with playrooms; opening the playrooms' wholly-glazed inner walls creates as much as 700m² of unlimited play area. Playrooms are connected with sliding doors so that spaces, children and activities can easily be united, which was envisaged as part of the kindergarten's design and pedagogy agenda.

Children in the Šmartno kindergarten spend at least two to three hours daily on average with a free choice of activity and company. This allows them to mix with peers from other groups and get to know younger and older children, as well as teachers from other groups. The interior design follows this philosophy of everyone everywhere: instead of eight similar playrooms, each room has different play equipment and learning environments. Some playrooms are more into science, others are better furnished for music and art, or sports, or just play. There are more than 65 activity corners children can freely choose from. The timeshare approach gives children the chance to enjoy an adjusted schedule according to their interests, and provides comparatively more access to play and learning activities in comparison to traditional kindergartens. The number of social contacts is also greater, which benefits the development of the youngsters' social skills, EQ and IQ. The staff was trained to make the best use of the kindergarten's specific design, and they are excited with the results and working conditions.

The core of the building is a multi-purpose central area with multifunctional rainbow-coloured stairs. These help children learn colours and numbers, while the side walls – blackboards – serve as a large canvas for children's art. Under the stairs there is storage space and a special « badger's den » with pillows where children can have their own calm retreat hidden from the rest of the more active areas. The cherry on top is the red slide, an endless attractor of play and physical exercise. Children love to slide down it instead of using the stairs, while to reach it they unknowingly overcome 22 stairs. The slide is a major passive element of exercise: children go down the slide 10–20 times each day on average. They slide alone and in groups of two or even three at a time.

Open Timeshare Kindergarten Šmartno

Design Agency : Arhitektura Jure Kotnik
Country : Slovenia

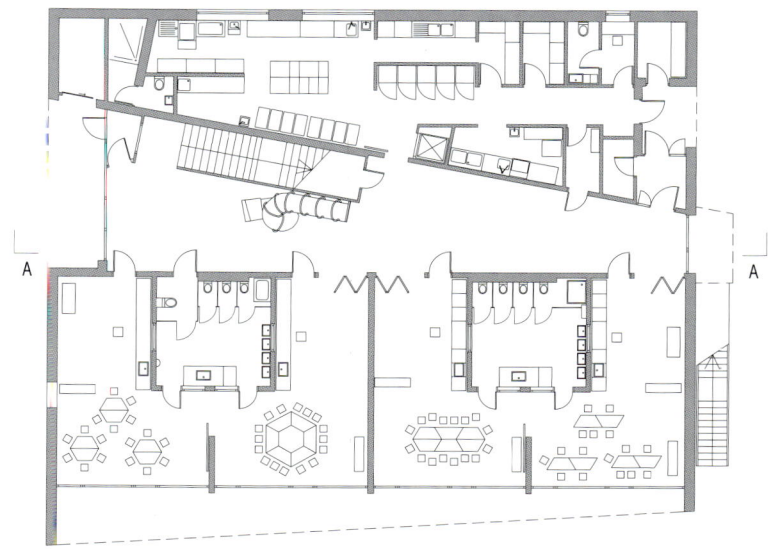

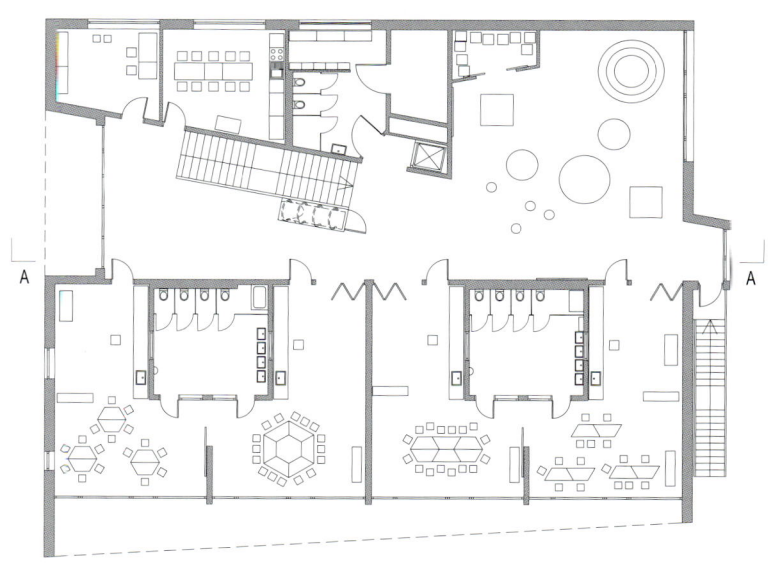

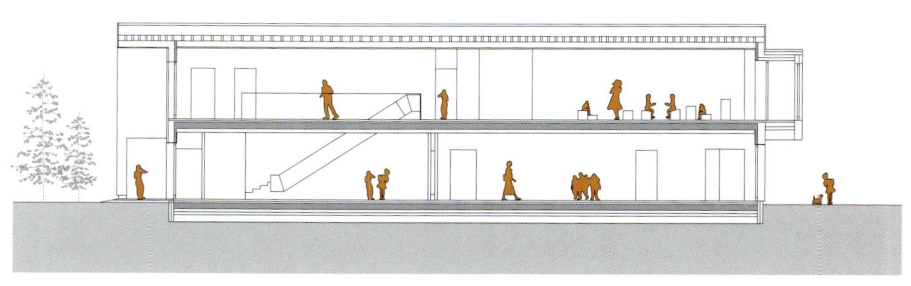

0 5 10

Open Timeshare Kindergarten Šmartno

Design Agency : Arhitektura Jure Kotnik
Country : Slovenia

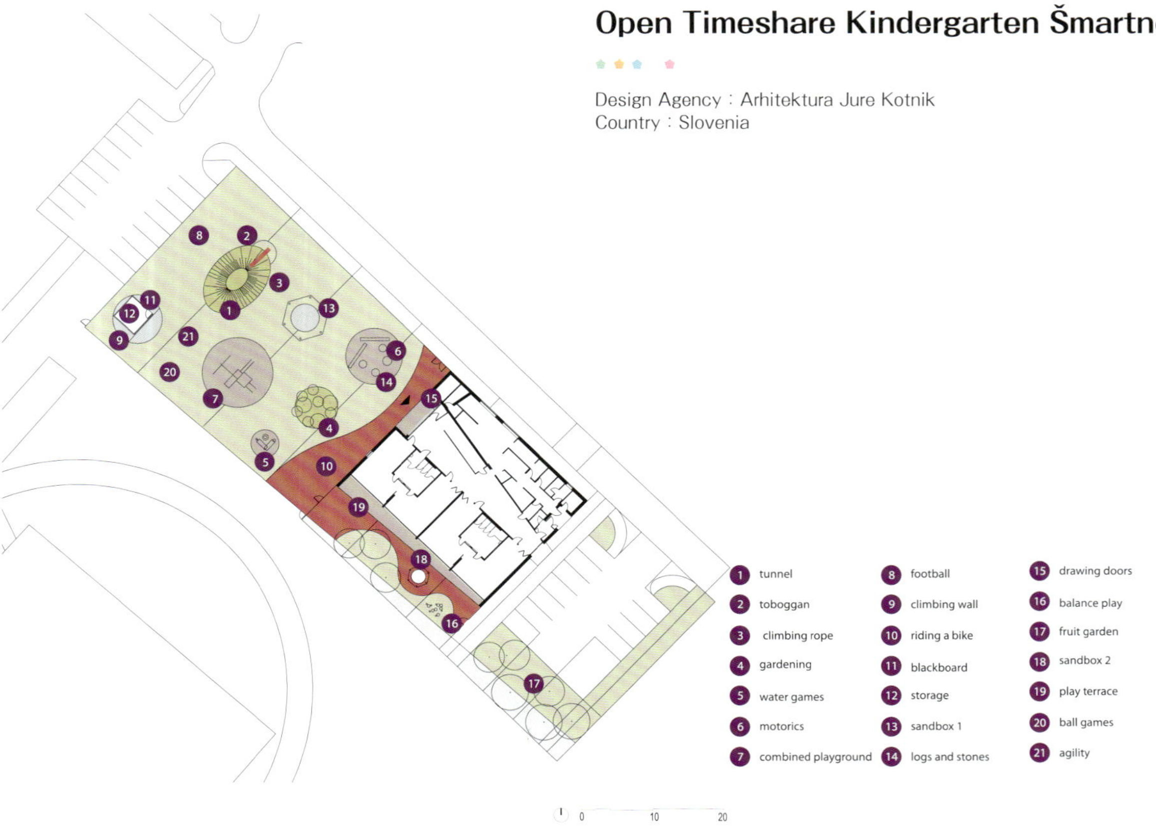

1 tunnel	8 football	15 drawing doors
2 toboggan	9 climbing wall	16 balance play
3 climbing rope	10 riding a bike	17 fruit garden
4 gardening	11 blackboard	18 sandbox 2
5 water games	12 storage	19 play terrace
6 motorics	13 sandbox 1	20 ball games
7 combined playground	14 logs and stones	21 agility

Open Timeshare Kindergarten Šmartno

Design Agency : Arhitektura Jure Kotnik
Country : Slovenia

Open Timeshare Kindergarten Šmartno

Design Agency : Arhitektura Jure Kotnik
Country : Slovenia

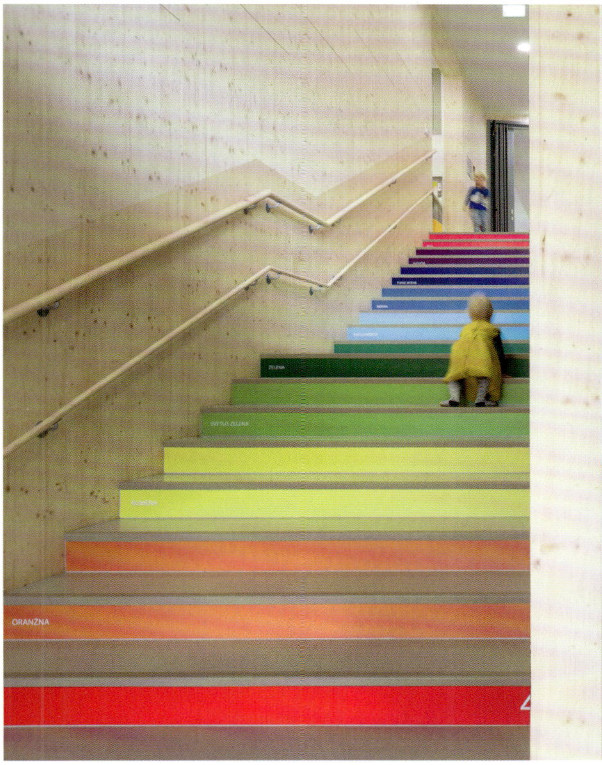
ZELENA
SVETLO ZELENA
ORANŽNA
4

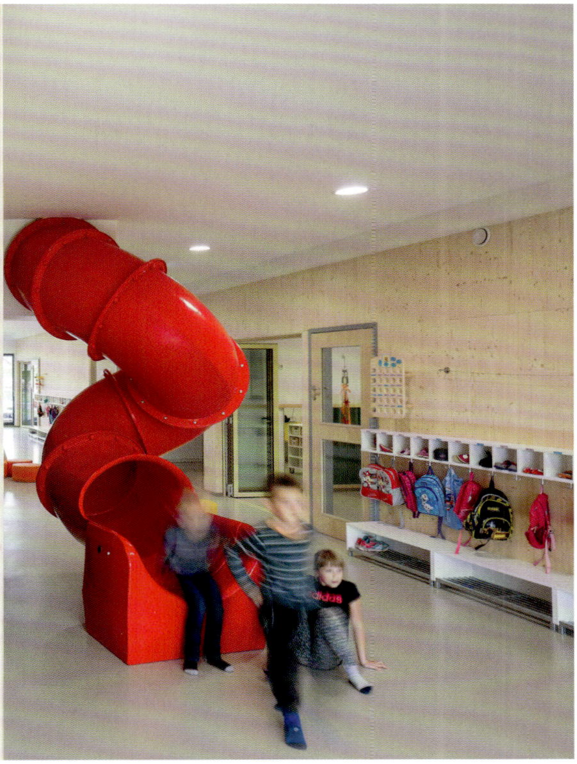

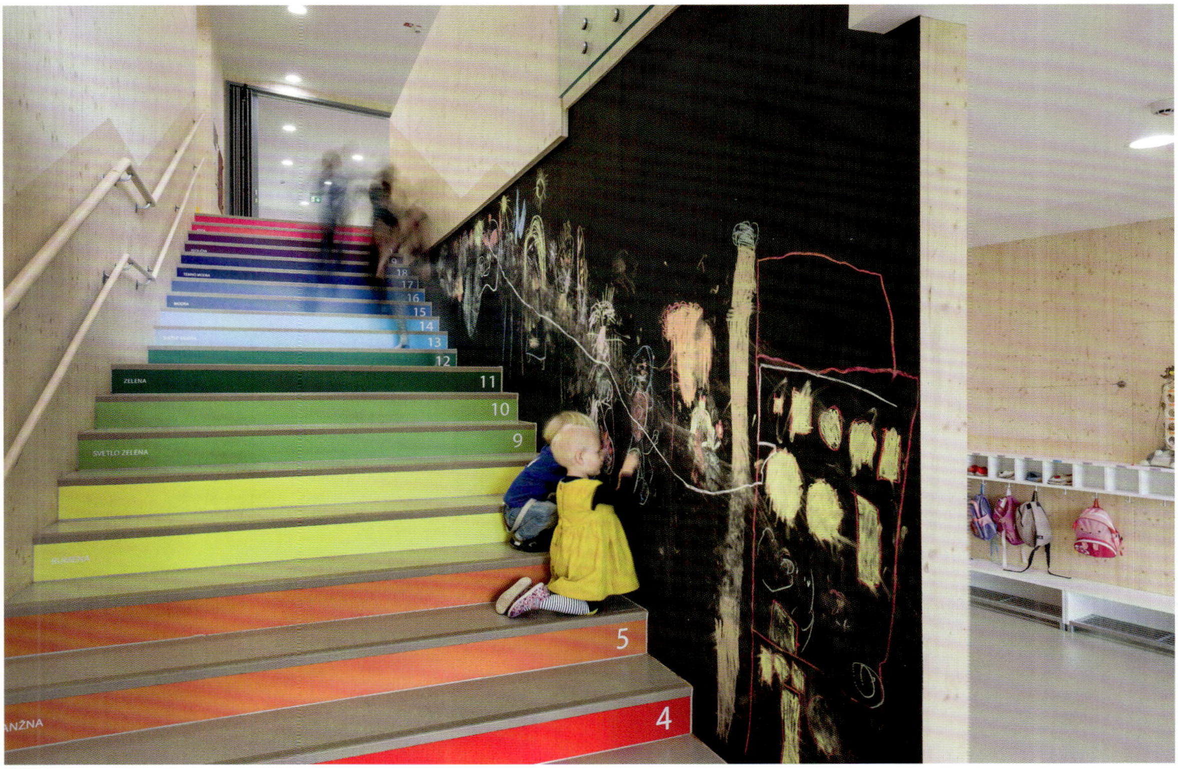
17
16
15
14
13
12
ZELENA
11
10
SVETLO ZELENA
9
5
ANŽNA
4

250

Open Timeshare Kindergarten Šmartno

Design Agency : Arhitektura Jure Kotnik
Country : Slovenia

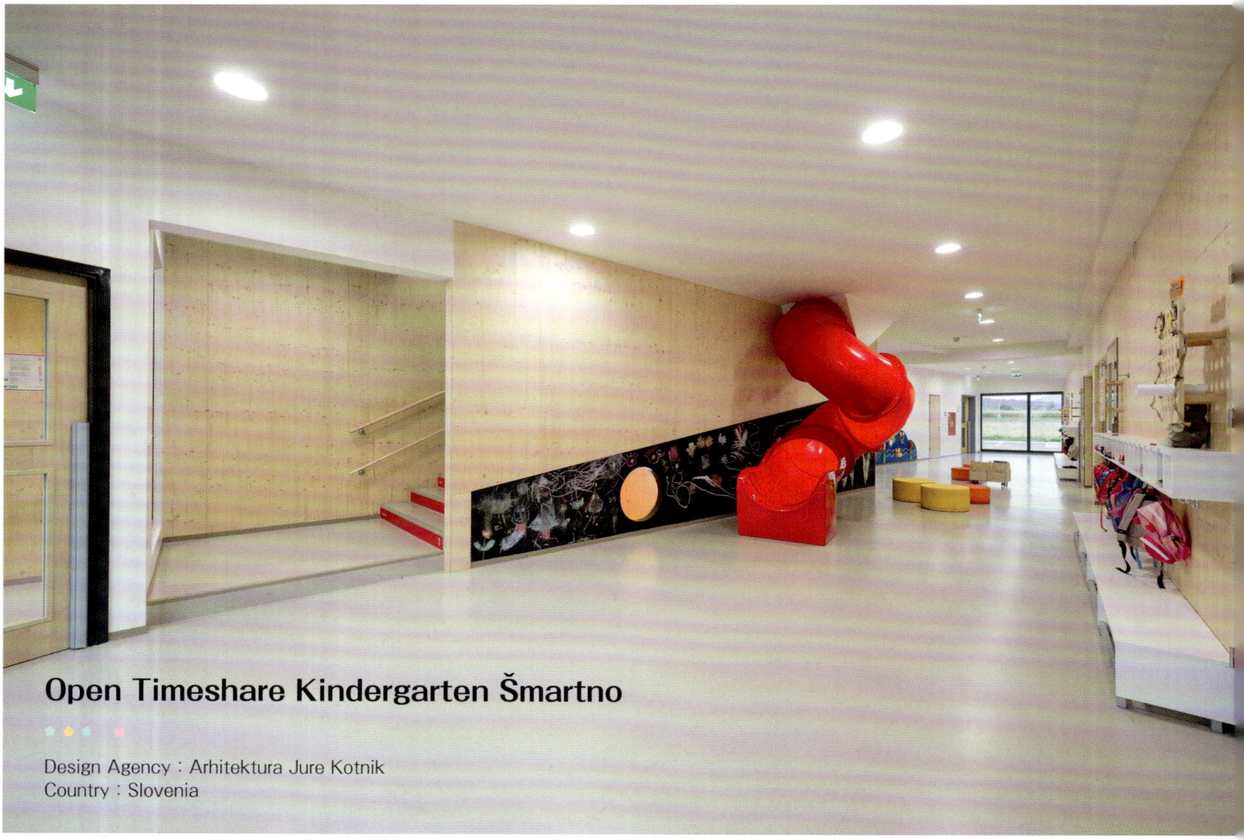

Open Timeshare Kindergarten Šmartno

Design Agency : Arhitektura Jure Kotnik
Country : Slovenia

254

Open Timeshare Kindergarten Šmartno

Design Agency : Arhitektura Jure Kotnik
Country : Slovenia

Architects : feld72 Architekten ZT GmbH
Country : Austria
Photographer : Hertha Hurnaus
Client : Municipality of Olang
Project Location : Olang, Italy

Educational Ensemble Terenten

The idea of the educational ensemble originated from a study in 2005, which involved the local community to develop a holistic concept for the village. Based on the original building of the 1970s, where the school and the kindergarten were housed together, a concept developed over the years which allows both facilities more space and interaction whilst at the same time integrating the existing village library. The educational ensemble opens itself to the village and vice versa – it becomes part of everyday life.

Educational Ensemble Terenten

Architects : felc72 Architekten ZT GmbH
Country : Austria

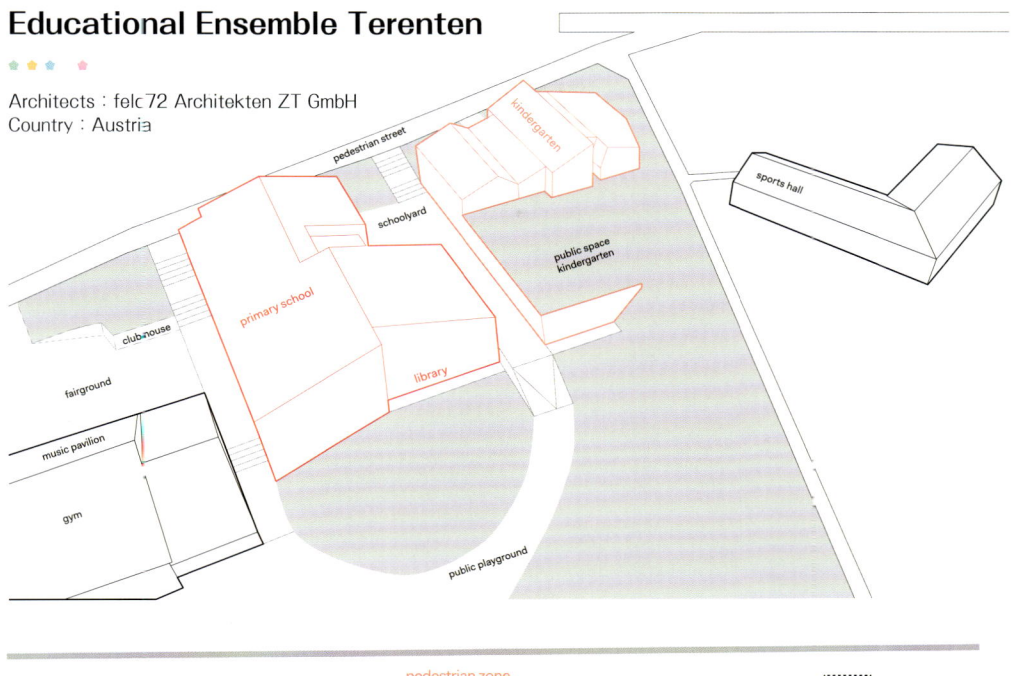

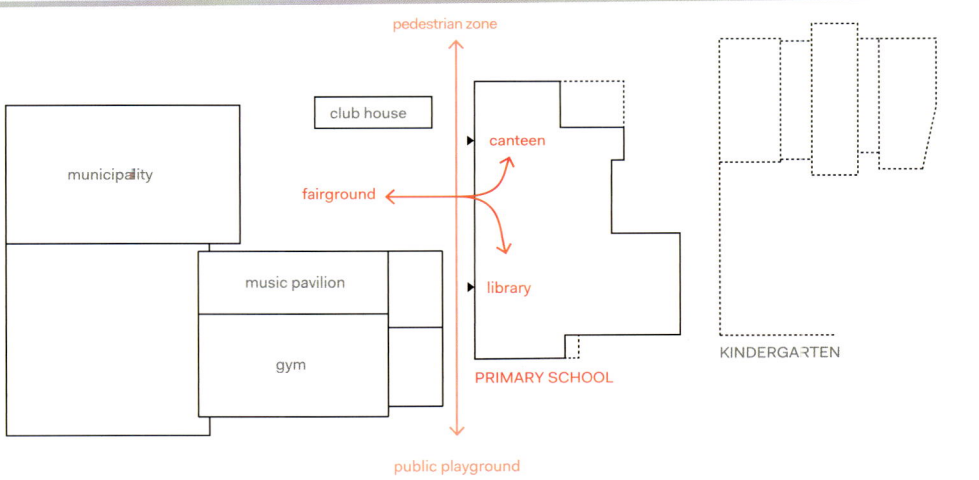

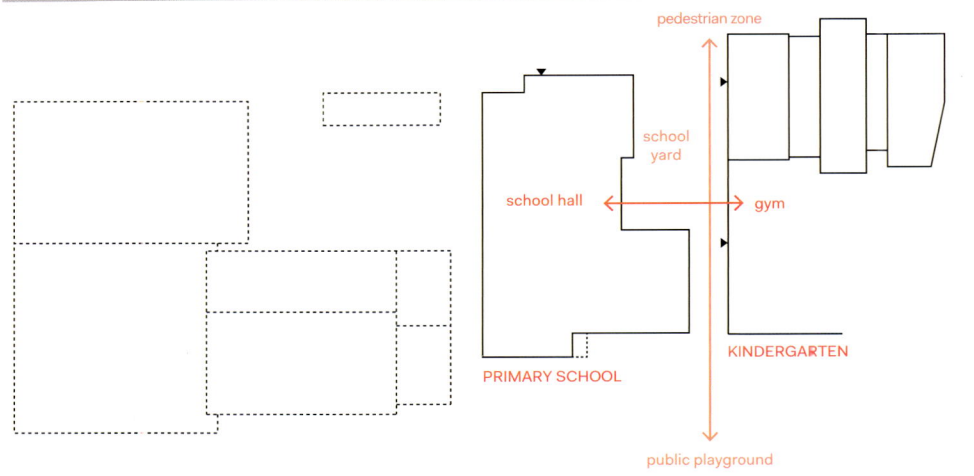

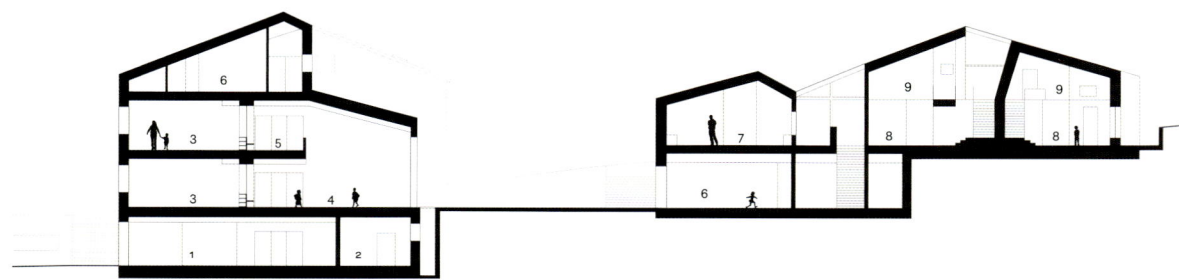

Educational Ensemble Terenten

● ● ● ●

Architects : feld72 Architekten ZT GmbH
Country : Austria

Primary school
1. canteen
2. kitchen
3. classroom
4. school hall
5. gallery
6. attic

Kindergarten
6. multi purpose room
7. staff
8. group room
9. gallery group room

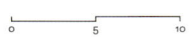

Educational Ensemble Terenten

Architects : feld72 Architekten ZT GmbH
Country : Austria

264

Educational Ensemble Terenten

Architects : feld72 Architekten ZT GmbH
Country : Austria

Kindergarten Niederolang

The kindergarten illustrates the local mesh of tradition, contemporary life and nature within the slowly grown village structure. The timber building is surrounded by a solid wall, embracing the garden in a friendly gesture. The wall is of varied materiality and volume – it shelters, frames, invites to play and presents insights and outlooks. The building itself remains clear and yet diverse. The spatial concept enables attractive variations in the educational approach – from small areas for retreat to rooms which can be used either connected or individually.

Architects : feld72 Architekten ZT GmbH
Country : Austria
Photographer : Hertha Hurnaus
Client : Municipality of Olang
Project Location : O ang, Italy

Kindergarten Niederolang

Architects : feld72 Architekten ZT GmbH
Country : Austria

269

Architects : CCDSTUDIO
Country : Italy
Creative Director : Luca CIAFFONI, Michele CIUTTI, Antonio DI MARCANTONIO
Photographer : Fabio MANTOVANI
Dimensions : 1625m²
Client : KARABAK7 – COOP.VA SOC. SOCIETA' DOLCE
Project Location : Municipality of OZZANO DELL'EMILIA (BO)

New Daycare And Childhood Center

This Center for Childhood created for the call about project financing between the municipality of Ozzano del' Emilia, near Bologna, and the Consorzio Karabak7. The design works start after the competition for this propose project financing. CCDSTUDIO designed the architecture spaces for the group of Coop companies that won the project financing. These two subjects, joined in a common aim, have provided for the new spaces of public facilities that were represented by two main building: the new Center Chidhood District and the Offices for the Municipal Police and the Administration. The Childhood spaces are composed to a Kindergarten for 69 babies and a Primary for 112 children, with a Center for families added. Therefore the project has different architectural scales by his program and by consequent dimension. The design, indeed, start from an urban draw to mark in the two different building the specific sign in which the program is implemented: the first, the School, that has inside a kindergarten, a nursery and a caycare center, is elongated on the flat land in only one elevation. Differently, the new building for the offices was been built on three floors in elevation. Formal research about the sense of architectural unity involve contrast and complementing elements like a leitmotiv for the entire project. Episodic holes create linear filaments that dig into the massive facades allowing deep punctures of glass transparency that mark the volumes. Modular lighting in the form of terracotta strips is located at the front of the two buildings. The horizontal lines enhance the urban planning of the site. This symbol announces a linking and union to a collective identity in the city of Ozzano.

New Daycare And Childhood Center

Architects : CCDSTUDIO
Country : Italy

Elevation

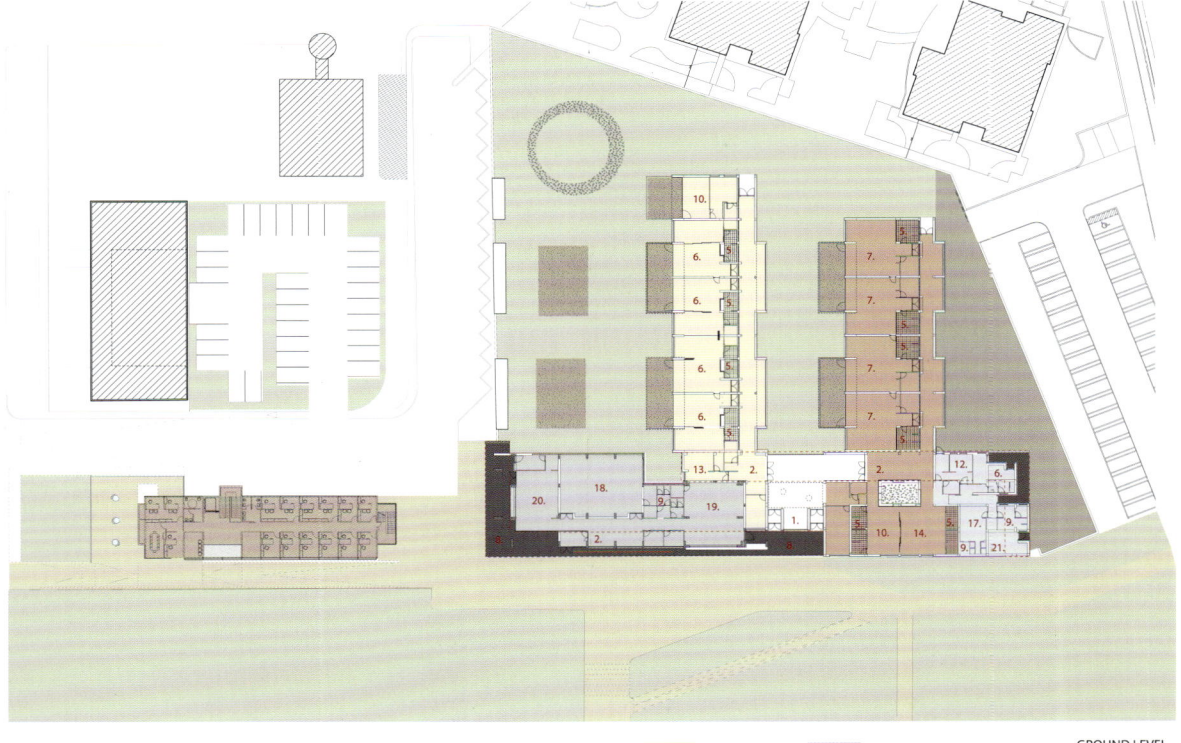

1. acceptance
2. hall
3. kindergarten office
4. nursery office
5. lavatory
6. classroom kindergarten
7. classroom nursery
8. portico
9. wc
10. workroom
11. hallway
12. kitchen
13. kitchenette
14. refectory
15. patio
16. store room
17. dressing room
18. meeting room
19. toy library
20. center for elderly
21. local technical

kindergarten
nursery
services
center for families
offices for local authorities

GROUND LEVEL
N
0 5 10m

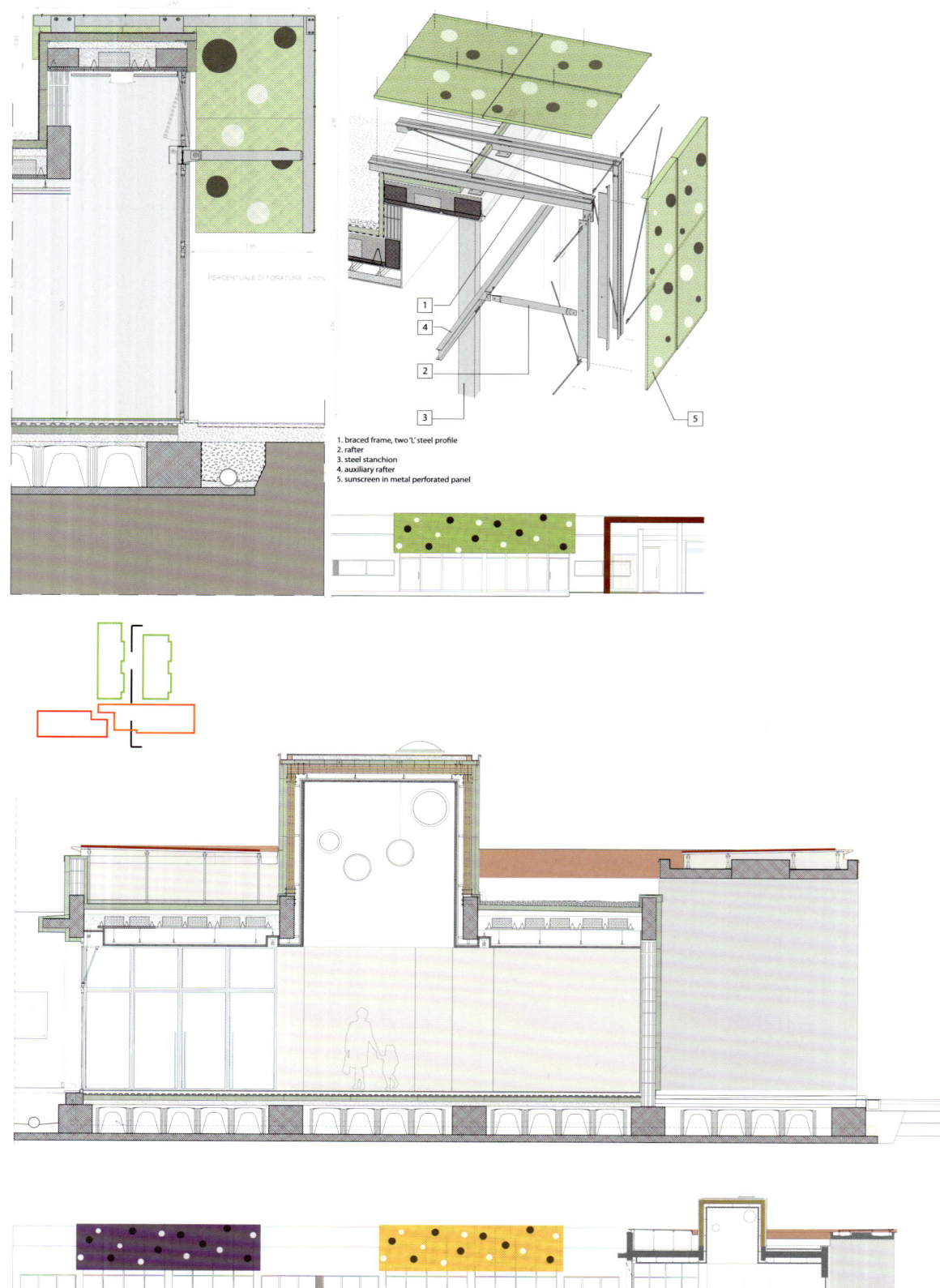

1. braced frame, two 'L' steel profile
2. rafter
3. steel stanchion
4. auxiliary rafter
5. sunscreen in metal perforated panel

New Daycare And Childhood Center

Architects : CCDSTUDIO
Country : Italy

New Daycare And Childhood Center

Architects : CCDSTUDIO
Country : Italy

New Daycare And Childhood Center

Architects : CCDSTUDIO
Country : Italy

New Daycare And Childhood Center

Architects : CCDSTUDIO
Country : Italy

281

New Daycare And Childhood Center

Architects : CCDSTUDIO
Country : Italy

283

Kindergarten 'BARBAPAPÀ'

The project of Kindergarten "Barbapapà" was designed to a notice competition for project financing, in 2006, proposed by Vignola's municipality. The program consisted in the space for 60 children divided in four classroom. The area is located on the border of urban development, on the hill up the city, not so much far to the historical centre. The natural environment induced specific assessments to preserve this atypical part of the landscape in the Emilia Romagna's region. The project aimed to be an architectural expression of mature consciousness about the sustainable themes. This value was found in the all possible relationships with surroundings. The architectural project start to this point and express this principal theme in all his part, to transmit the sustainable value to all his young guests.

A summary is proposed in the next points:

Reduce the impact of the volume. A green vegetable plan was raised from the ground to accept below it, the protected spaces for the children, and to reduce the visual impact of the volume, entered in the hill, from the urban street below. Control the comfort inside. The green deck ensures to maintain a good thermal insulation, to preserve the environmental comfort with a terrain package placed on top of the roof's wood structure.

Capture natural resource from the environment. The satisfying of daily needs is pursued through natural resources. The appropriate glass's openings, used for all the length of the facade, are studied to permit at the filtered sun to enter properly during different times of day and to heat the space inside.

Other resource heat was captured by two different devices: geothermal probes placed inside bulkhead trigger an heat exchange between the ground and thermal pump; photovoltaic panels are putted in a compartment on the metal roof in copper that cover the other spaces of the kindergarten; the rainwater reused for the irrigation and for the sewage water in the bathrooms.

Architects : CCDSTUDIO
Country : Italy
Creative Director : Luca CIAFFONI, Michele CIUTTI, Antonio DI MARCANTONIO
Photographer : Fabio MANTOVANI
Dimensions : 1158m²
Client : VIGNOLAZEROSEI - COOP.VA SOC. SOCIETA' DOLCE
Project Location : Municipality of VIGNOLA (MO)

Kindergarten 'BARBAPAPÀ'

Architects : CCDSTUDIO
Country : Italy

1. public entrance
2. service entrance
3. public parking
4. private parking
5. rest area
6. storage strollers
7. solar and photovoltaic panel
8. green roof
9. paved area
10. garden of sand
11. garden vegetable
12. playground
13. natural arena
14. garden of flowers
15. native vegetation

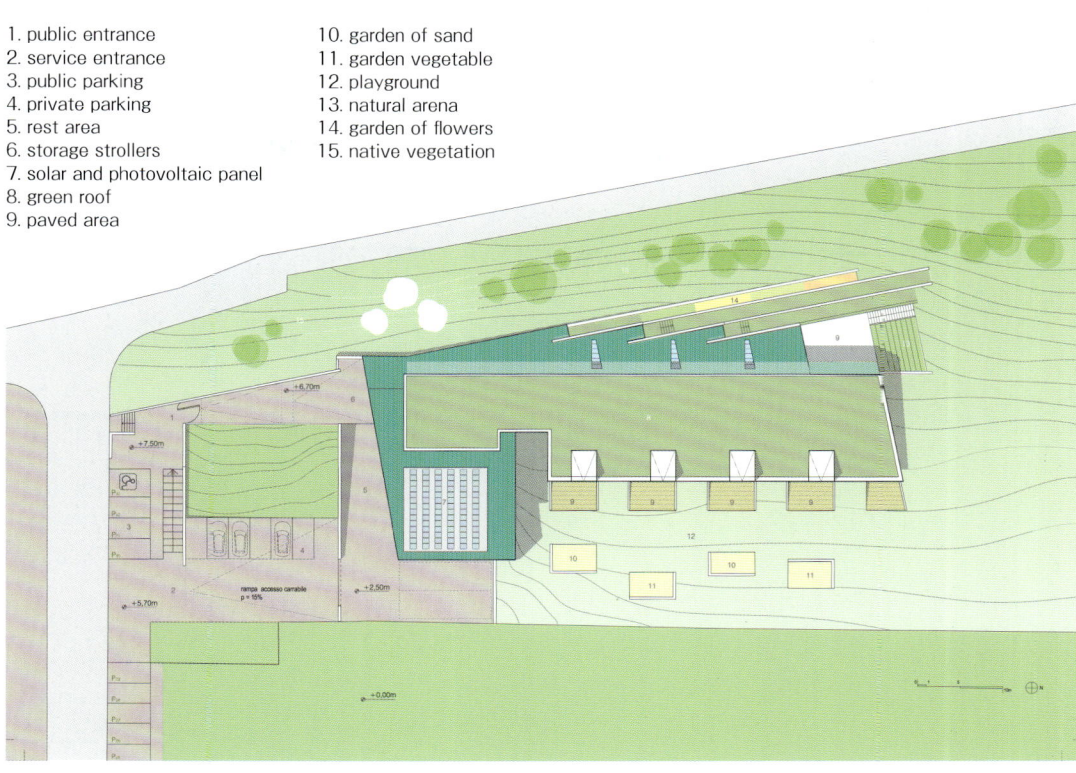

1. trail access
2. entrance
3. waiting
4. office administration
5. restroom
6. center for childrens and parents
7. staircase and elevator
8. common area
9. workroom
10. classroom
11. natural arena
12. emergency escape

Level 0 - Ground floor

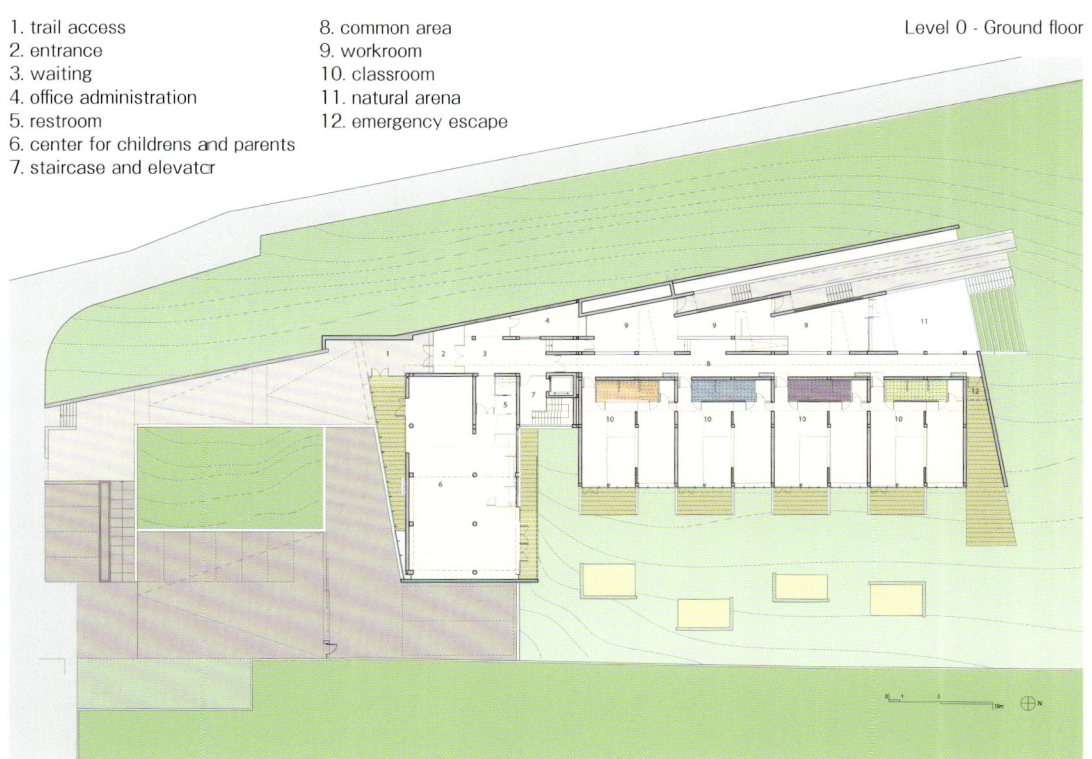

Kindergarten 'BARBAPAPÀ'

Architects : CCDSTUDIO
Country : Italy

289

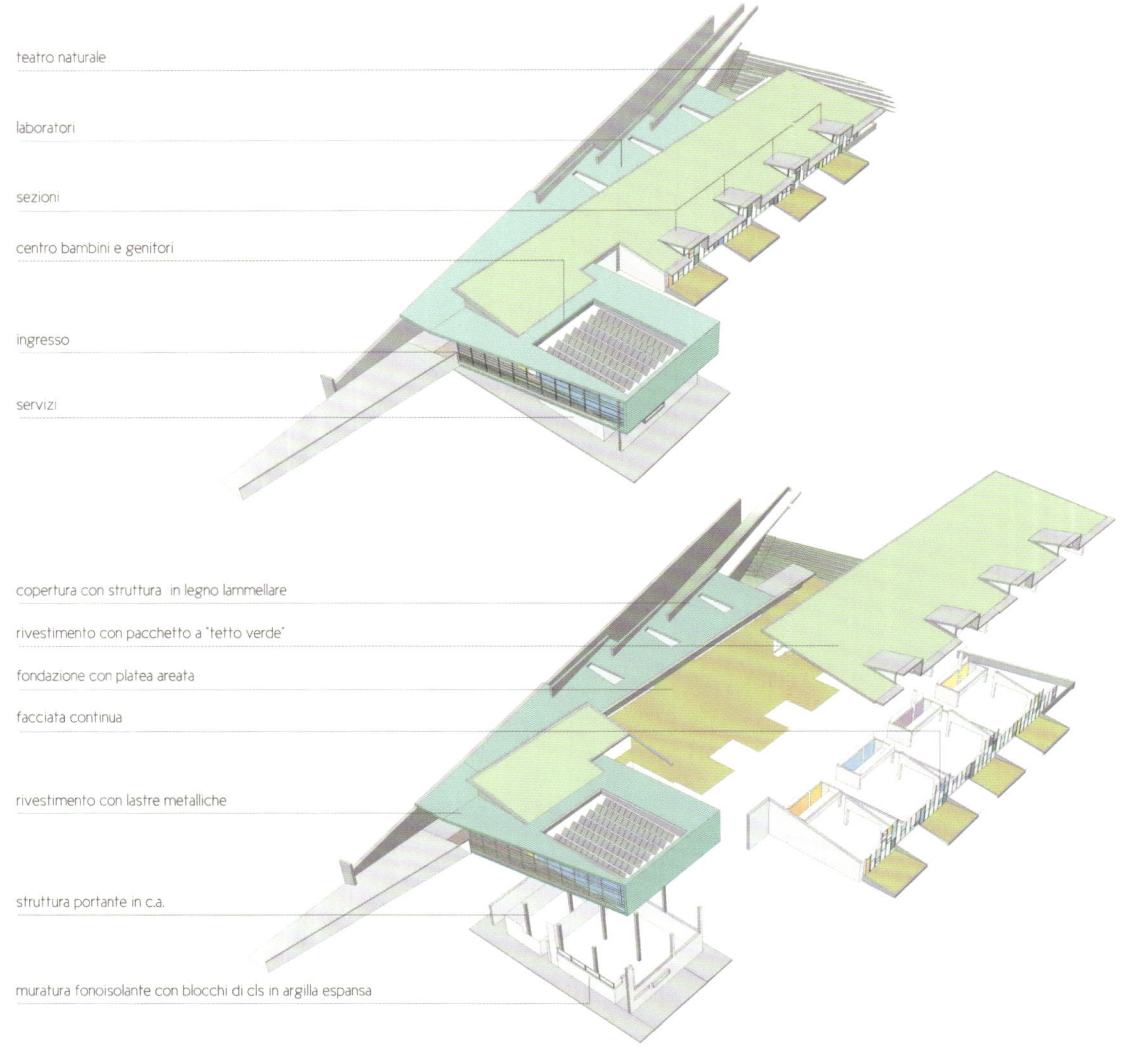

Kindergarten 'BARBAPAPÀ'

Architects : CCDSTUDIO
Country : Italy

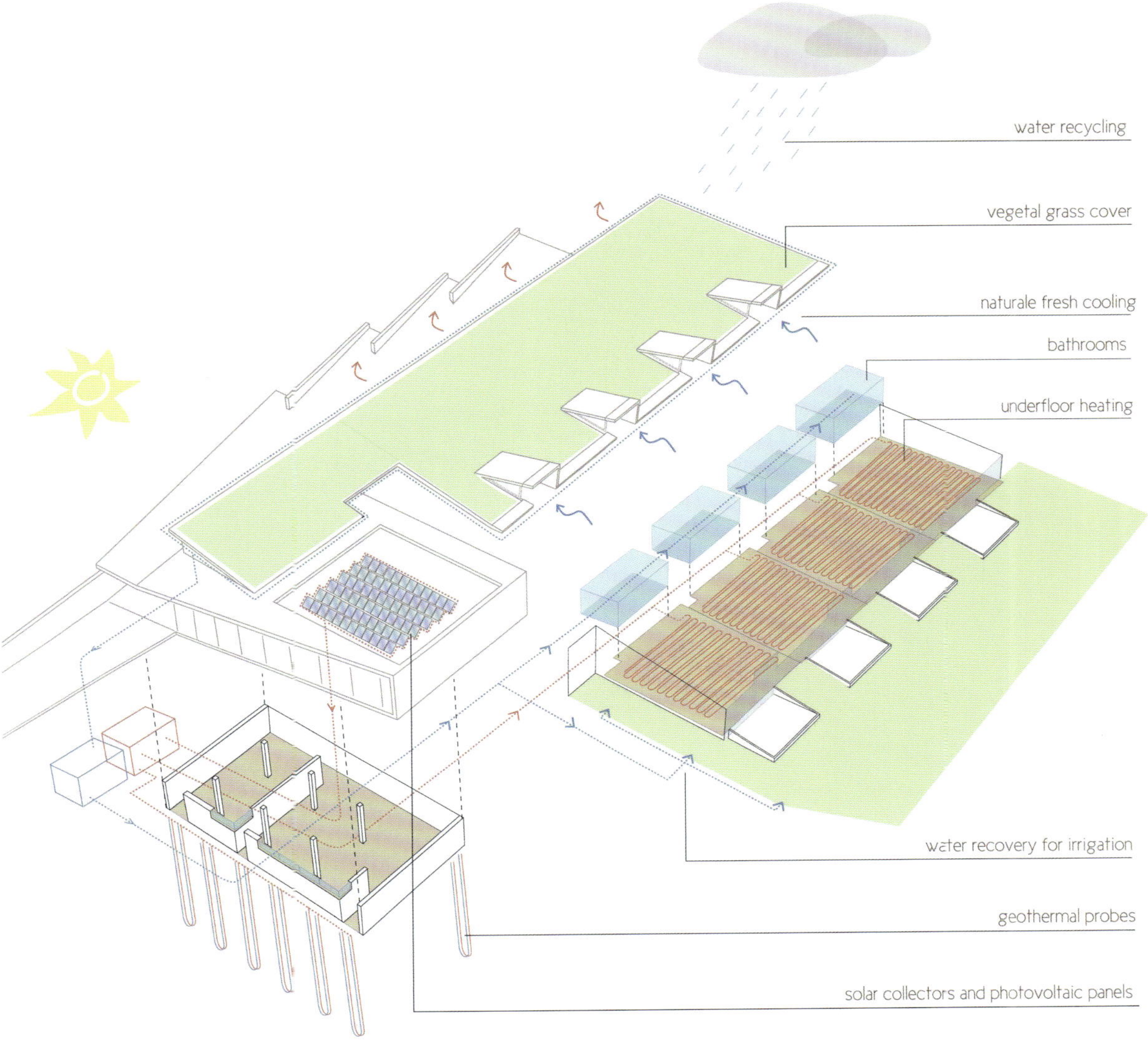

water recycling

vegetal grass cover

naturale fresh cooling

bathrooms

underfloor heating

water recovery for irrigation

geothermal probes

solar collectors and photovoltaic panels

Kindergarten 'BARBAPAPÀ'

Architects : CCDSTUDIO
Country : Italy

293

Kindergarten 'BARBAPAPÀ'

Architects : CCDSTUDIO
Country : Italy

Kindergarten 'BARBAPAPÀ'

Architects : CCDSTUDIO
Country : Italy

4th Public Nursery of the Municipality of Glyfada

The concept of the project was to design a building that would relate to the scale of its users while also introducing a new typology, that of the urban village. The main module draws inspiration from archetypal drawing of a house as perceived by a child. By replicating the basic module thrice, the classroom unit is created. The nursery school was designed so that all the classrooms have three open sides. As a consequence, the arrangement of the classrooms is organized around a central courtyard while also formed by smaller atriums.

Additionally, we intended to give prominence to the construction method of prefabrication. Prefabrication, one of the conditions of the architectural competition the firm entered, also defined the final form of the building, as the basic module would have to be transported on a truck.

We attempted to employ rather common materials and construction methods in order to create a more complicated structure with a small energy footprint. The exterior walls were constructed 10cm thick allowing us to maximize the available interior area and were cladded, along with the roofs, with exterior wall insulation.

Thus, by taking also into consideration the construction of wooden pergolas along the careful placement of the windows on the exterior walls, the building is sustainable providing comfort to the children. On the other hand, we hope that the vegetation will become a quintessential element of the design as large Platanus trees will provide shade to the interior courtyard while other tree species will highlight the seasonal changes.

Architects : Klab Architecture
Principal Architect : Konstantinos Labrinopoulos
Project Architect : Veronica Vasileiou
Design Team : Konstantinos Labrinopoulos, Veronika Vasileiou, Petra Xynidou (intern), Myrto Lantza (intern), Kelly Kagka
Country : Greece
Photographer : Mariana Bisti
Client : Municipality of Glyfada, Athens, Greece
Project Location : Pyrgou Str. Glyfada, Athens, Greece

4th Public Nursery of the Municipality of Glyfada

Architects : Klab Architecture
Country : Greece

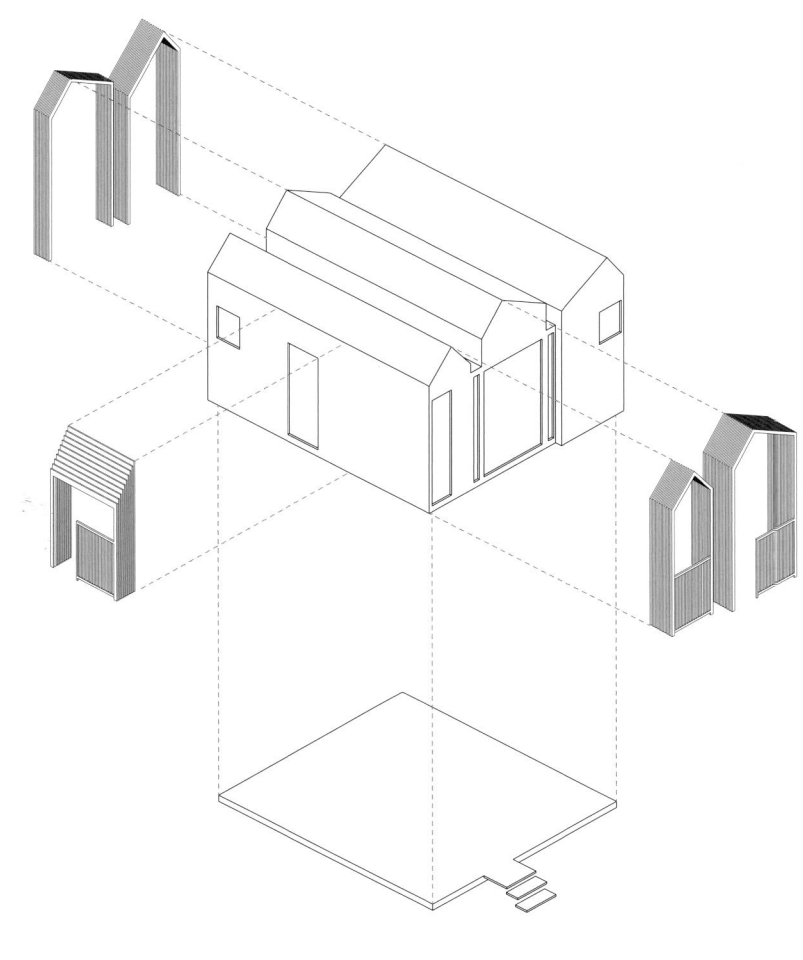

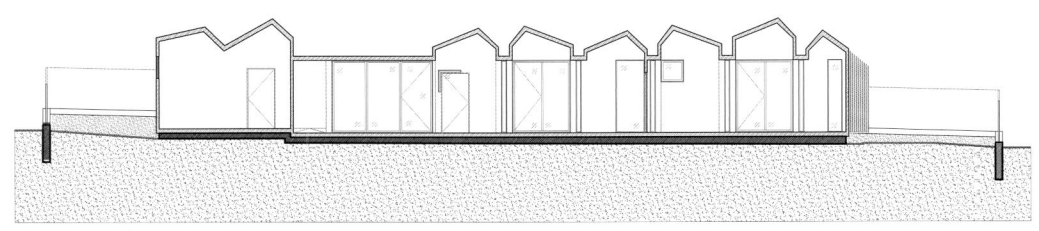

SECTION A-A'

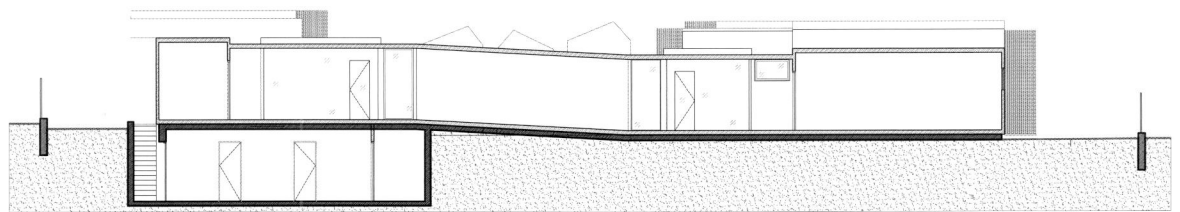

SECTION B-B'

4th Public Nursery of the Municipality of Glyfada

Architects : Klab Architecture
Country : Greece

4th Public Nursery of the Municipality of Glyfada

Architects : Klab Architecture
Country : Greece

305

Nursery in Guastalla

Kindergartens are important places because that is where children begin to explore the world and begin to know it. In such places, there should be natural light, as the sun's messenger, natural materials to enhance tactile sensitivity, colors to help children imagine and draw landscapes. There, nature is seen as the clock of the seasons. Flowers and colors depend on the seasons and give us a sense of nature's rhythms. This is what the Guastalla Kindergarten is: built with laminated wood, and set on a reinforced concrete base, it guarantees 100% seismic security and 100% environmental safety. These are two factors which are non-negotiable.

It was built with some urgency, and it was so because it also stands as a symbol of the pride of the region of Emilia where, in 2012, an earthquake destroyed the previous kindergarten. The Guastalla Kindergarten was built to replace it. It was a collective effort, including the city council, teachers, families, and not least of all, the children.

The building is one of the first attempts to introduce environmental education. It produces energy from the sun, collects rainwater to irrigate the garden, and uses natural light. This is all a fundamental part of the educational project, which is that of raising new generations of individuals who will know how to face the environmental challenges of tomorrow.

Architects : Mario Cucinella
Country : Italy
Design Agency : Mario Cucinella Architects
Photographer : Moreno Maggi
Dimensions : 1400m²
Client : Guastalla Municipality
Project Location : Guastalla, Reggio Emilia, Italy

Nursery in Guastalla

Architects : Mario Cucinella
Country : Italy

SEZIONE E-E

SEZIONE F-F

SEZIONE G-G

SEZIONE H-H

Nursery in Guastalla

Architects : Mario Cucinella
Country : Italy

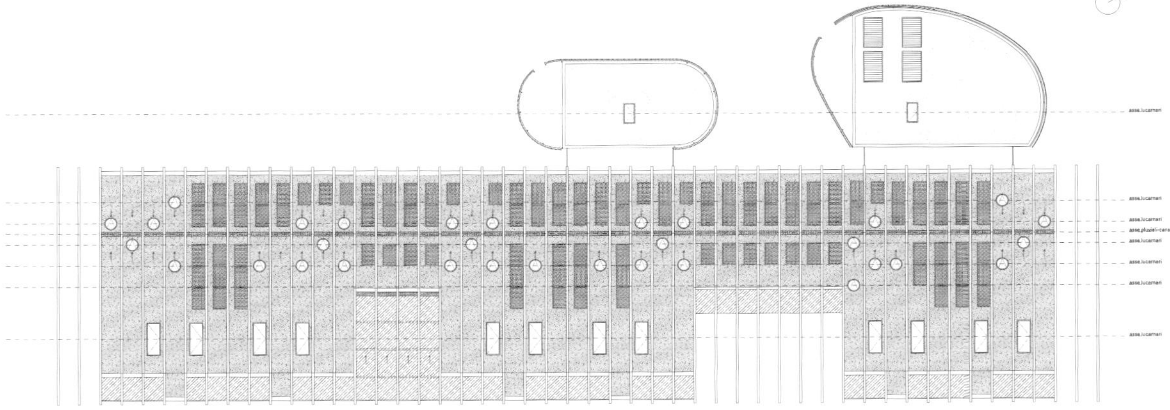

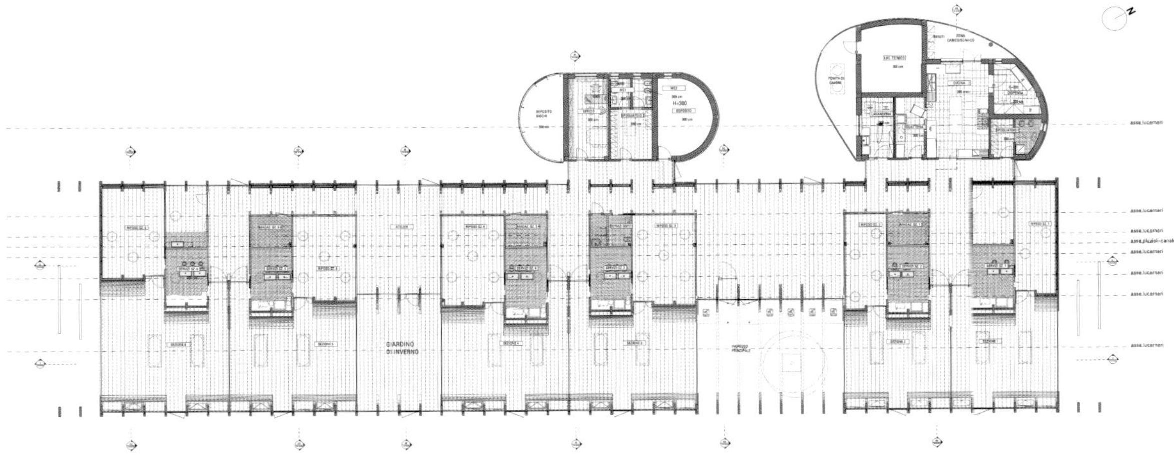

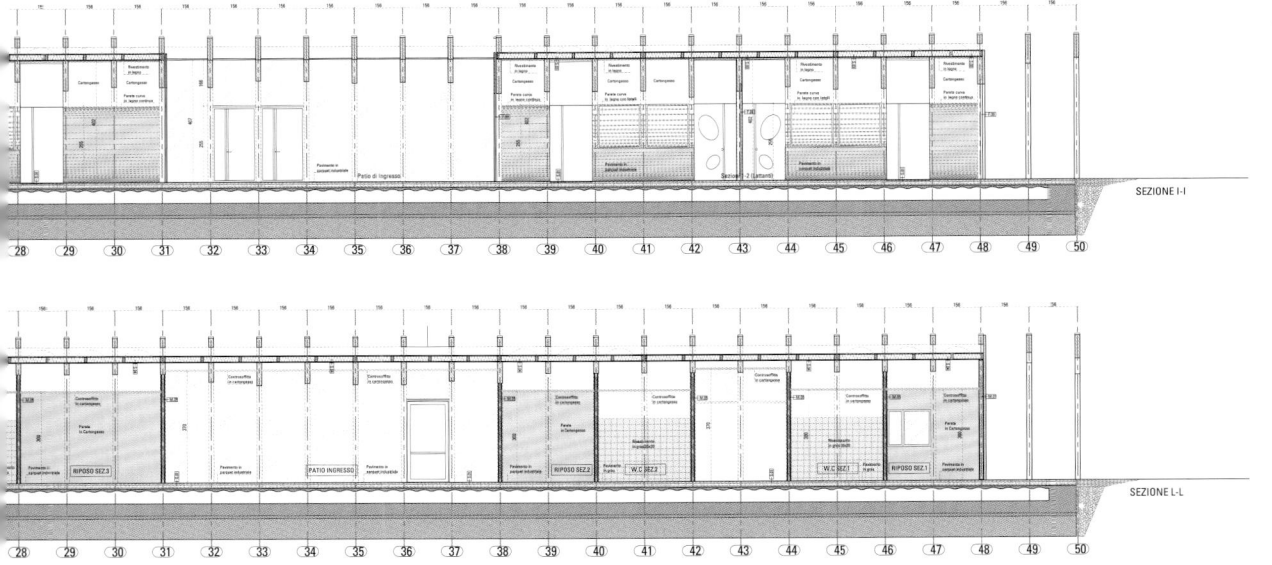

Nursery in Guastalla

Architects : Mario Cucinella
Country : Italy

Nursery in Guastalla

Architects : Mario Cucinella
Country : Italy

316

Nursery in Guastalla

Architects : Mario Cucinella
Country : Italy

Nursery in Guastalla

Architects : Mario Cucinella
Country : Italy

319

Kindergarten in Dobrín

The site the community decided to develop for a kindergarten for 30 children is one of the nicest in the village. It is a vacant lot at the historical village green with a view to the river and a corresponding area for a garden.

The basic vision was to situate the kindergarten in the vicinity, in symbiosis with the country and village. The formal concept was developed complying with the historical concept of vernacular architecture. Colour and material design builds on the local genius loci reflected in the 'earthy' character of the building. In terms of abstraction, the building is based on the concept of a classic country house with a hip roof. Vernacular elements are also used on the facade that is rich with statuary referring to decorativeness of traditional architecture in the area. The sculptor is Jiri Vorel who has personal bond to this location.

The kindergarten in Dobrin is a return to the world of fairy-tales, to the world of children. It respects their visions and wishes; it should resemble a small 'cottage' that provides a harmony, warmth, and possibility to have a good romp. The spatial concept of the interior layout works with openness as much as possible and identifies itself as different compared with usually sterile Czech kindergartens. A child can scrawl over a wall and not suffer for doing so. A child becomes the master of the space it may freely transform. No rules exist ordering how the space should be treated, just a framework whose atmosphere the users establish for themselves. The kindergarten will keep on developing and transforming following this concept of understanding.

The kindergarten is surrounded by a garden with fruit trees positioned parallel with the east border of the lot. It is a one-story building of a rectangular footprint. The roof is a distinguished architectural and identifying element. At the north side, it is a classical hip roof with a pitch 35°; towards the south, it slowly pitches down towards one wall. Rafters are timber; the structure reflects the span. Approximately 8 m from the north gable the pitch abruptly changes establishing a clerestory window letting southern daylight in the children's playroom. Where possible, the interior opens up to the attic below the rafters. The roof is decked elsewhere in the attic.

The building meets conditions for a construction in an inundation area. This concept projects in the technical design and selected materials as well as the interior concept. The building is founded on mass-concrete continuous strips and isolated footings. Vertical outer and internal loadbearing walls are ceramic block to resist potential flooding. Interior non-bearing walls are ceramic brick. Window and door openings in vertical walls are designed to resist flooding or allowing for easy replacement for new ones. Roofing is copper colour aluminium sheet.

Author : ATELIER 8000 / Martin Krupauer, Jiri Stritecky (died 2012)
Co-author : Pavel Kvintus, Co-operation Jiri Vorel(sculptures)
Design Agency : ATELIER 8000
Country : Czech Republic
Photographer : Ondrej Bouška
Client : Dobrin Municipality
Project Location : Dobrin, Czech Republic, Europe

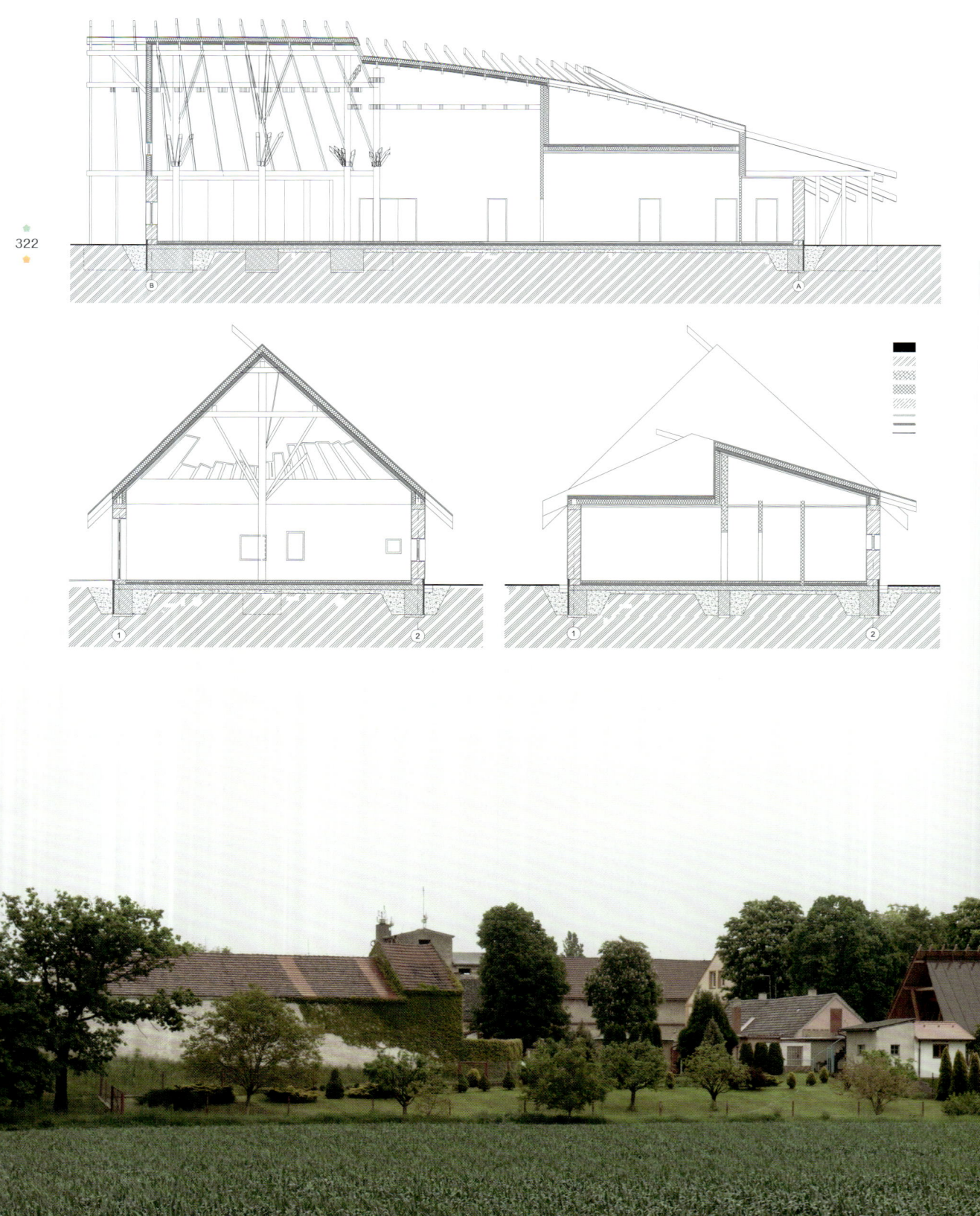

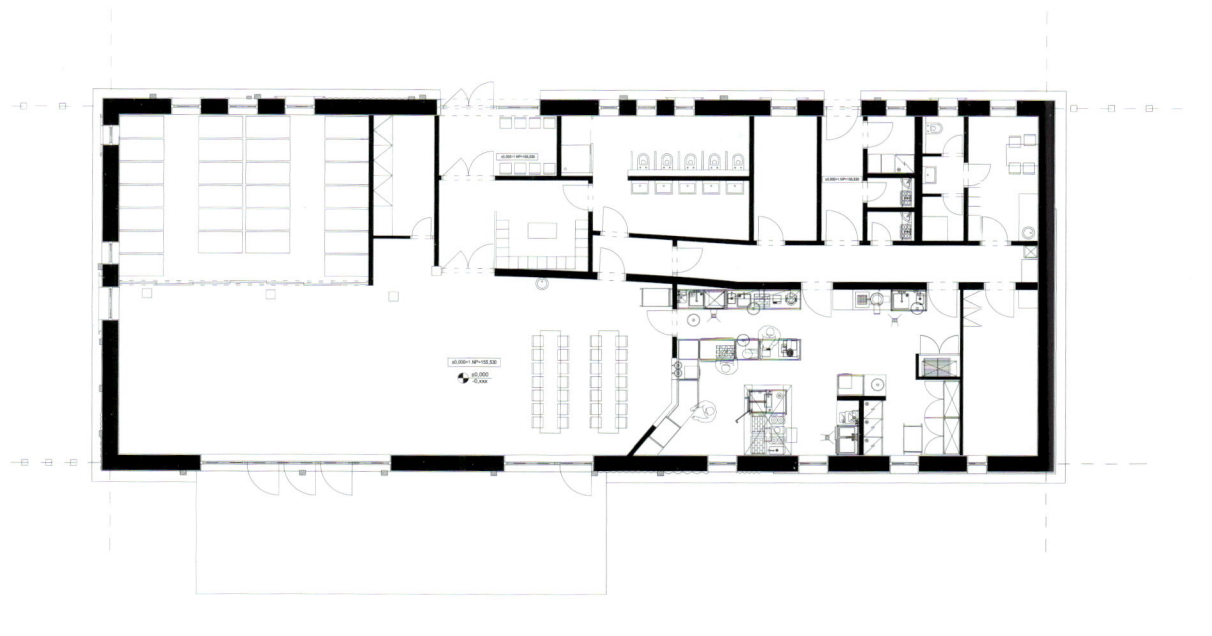

Kindergarten in Dobrín

Design Agency : ATELIER 8000
Country : Czech Republic

Kindergarten in Dobrín

● ● ● ●

Design Agency : ATELIER 8000
Country : Czech Republic

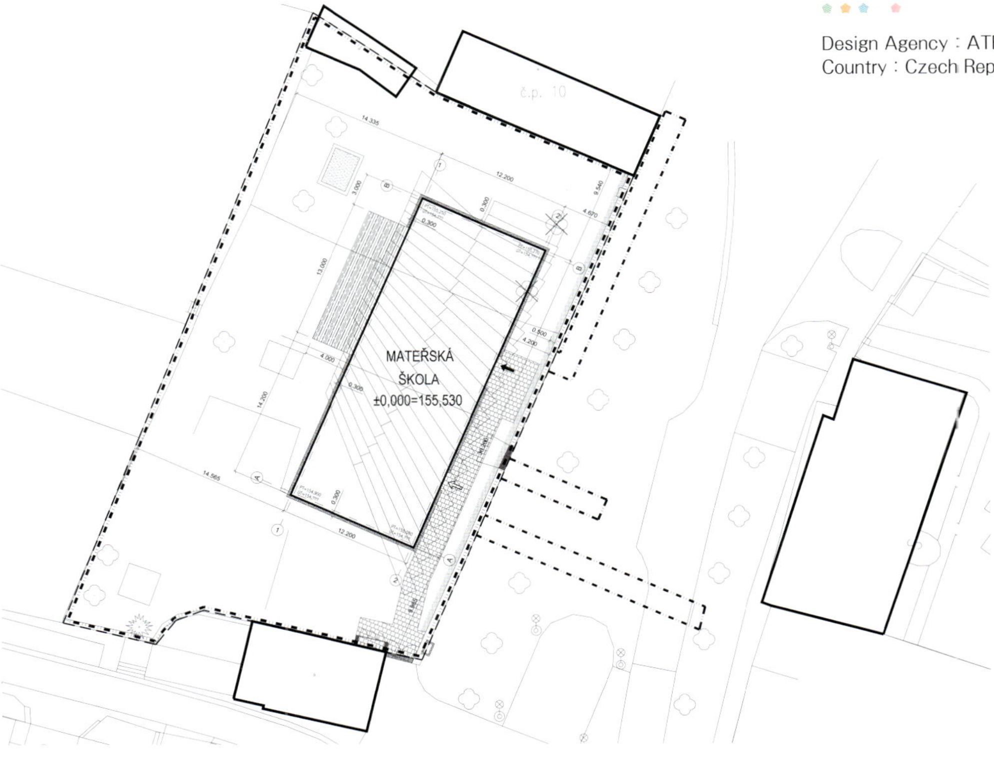

Kindergarten in Dobrín

Design Agency : ATELIER 8000
Country : Czech Republic

Kindergarten in Dobrín

Design Agency : ATELIER 8000
Country : Czech Republic

Nursery Pollenfeld

Pollenfeld, a small community in Upper-Bavaria, Germany, needed a new nursery. In a little competition, KÜHNLEIN Architektur has won the first prize and was assigned to realize the project. The brief was to preserve the fruit trees in the front of the area, so the new building is situated in the back. For having different places for outdoor activities, the children can use the stone-flagged atrium ore the fruit orchard. Adequate the idea of a wooden pavilion between the fruit trees. The facade is opened to the atrium and the trees with large windows. The use of ecological and sustainable products for the children is self-evident. The stringent German regulations for energy consumption are very well fulfilled. With the grill for sunscreen and slight openings for ventilation, the structure is an excellent example for a low-tec building.

Architects: Michael Kühnlein jun.
Country: Germany
Design Agency: KÜHNLEIN Architektur
Photographer: Erich Spahn
Project Location: Pollenfeld, Bavaria

Nursery Pollenfeld

Architects : Michael Kühnlein jun.
Country : Germany

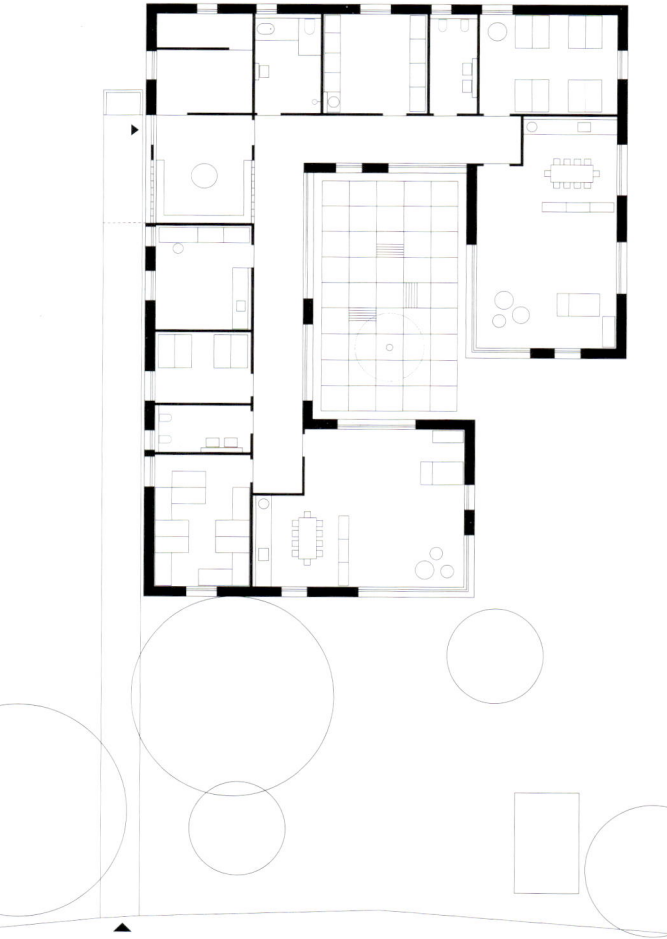

Nursery Pollenfeld

Architects : Michael Kühnlein jun.
Country : Germany

Nursery Pollenfeld

Architects : Michael Kühnlein jun.
Country : Germany

Architects : Vincent Parreira
Country : France
Design Agency : Atelier Architecture Vincent Parreira AAVP
Dimensions : 5186m²
Photography : Luc Boegly
Client : Aménagement 77 for La Ville de Montévrain
Project Location : Region Ile-de-France

MON –School Group and Leisure Center Louis de Vion –Montévrain

The school is a particularly important place for young children: a place of learning, but also of socialization, more or less a second home where young children must be able to feel safe, make this world their own and begin developing their independence. For the neighborhood, the school is of course a facility, but also a familiar, reassuring presence, a discreet link with the Republic, and a melting pot. Louis de Vion welcomes 500 students in nursery and primary schools, includes a leisure center that opens to the outdoors, as part of the logic of sharing and optimization of the premises when they are unoccupied during extended vacation periods, weekends and evenings.

Though school architecture was codified under the administration of Jules Ferry or, closer to us, through the industrialization of "models" proposed by the ministry of education, henceforth it no longer follows fixed rules, having entered an era of modern eclecticism. Relying on the contrast between the large, smooth, white concrete surfaces and the volumes made of textured gray-stained wood designed according to a relief diamond motif, the architectural style of Louis de Vion is perhaps disconcerting for some, just as its rare openings toward the outside, like open work of moucharabiehs cut out of the concrete walls replicating this same diamond motif. Easily identified thanks to their vaulted ceilings, the entry halls of the two schools do not resemble the customary solemn entrances to the temples of education. They are more like troglodyte homes, the vernacular, from elsewhere, the possibility of a Greek island or a school field trip. The walls of the classrooms inside the building are raw concrete, a closeness to the material which is tempered by the presence of a patio, a microcosm inside a larger world, the one of the school, or the city, which can be seen through the diamond cut-outs. Light, filtered by the moucharabiehs, broken by wood awnings, colored through the large skylights in the school dining areas, penetrating through the fracture bearing the footbridge that links the primary school with the activity center, reaches into the furthest corners of the building. The roof, visible from the zones on the second level of the school complex, recreates a prairie, reconnecting, in a way with the land of the original site. Protruding technical elements are hidden in volumes clad in wood. The same pre-patinated wood cladding was utilized on all the wooden parts. Wherever possible, part of the volume of these protrusions has been reassigned to the students, as with the dormitories for example, or the doubling of the ceiling height, challenging them with new spatial experiences.

Near the entrance for the nursery schoolers or for the primary schoolers, a tricolor flag, required accessory of every public school, underscores with humor the cementing role played by the Republic. Once inside, children emerge from the family cocoon to enter into another world. Far from adulterated dream worlds on sale just a few hundred meters away, they enter another non standardized world, with shimmering reflections, rustling echoes, and oddities; a world blending the unexpected and zooming on the surprising, in an imaginary wilderness and the stimulating surroundings of the metropolis. It offers a way of learning to be curious through architecture, a first encounter with the mysteries of the wider world.

MON –School Group and Leisure Center Louis de Vion –Montévrain

Architects : Vincent Parreira
Country : France

341

MON –School Group and Leisure Center Louis de Vion –Montévrain

Architects : Vincent Parreira
Country : France

MON –School Group and Leisure Center Louis de Vion –Montévrain

Architects : Vincent Parreira
Country : France

345

Angela Davis school Bezons

* * * *

The construction of the new Angela Davis school in Bezons takes part in the creation of the new city center. The project, by its function of active urban facility is a key part of this city center. The goal of this construction is double: it must be a functionnal and sustainable public facility and also a milestone of this new neighbourhood. The school plot is an important link wetween the new center and the rest of the city. On the east side, the one story building with its vegetated roof evokes the roofs of the surrounding houses. The school integrates itself softly to the existing urban grid. The landscape is prolongated all along the plot to the South until the Edouard Vaillant street and come inside the school under the zinc North facade.

The stone elevation creates inaccessible terraces reminiscent of suspended dry stone gardens and creates the promontory of the elementary school courtyard. This mineral stratification reminds castles, an évoque un château fort, a reassuring and timeless building, full of nature. The new school has a urban facade on Francis de Pressensé path with transparency on ground floor and suspended zinc «box» on first floor.

The bridge over the entrance spans the planted walkway which is integrated to the building as a natural protection and presence behind the facade. The rows of high plane trees on South and North are preserved, prolonging the park on E. vaillant street. On the secondary path, the facade is carefully designed with a succession of aluminum vertical pieces, playing with sunlight.

The entrance space is large and sheltered, shared between infant and elementary school. With the nature coming inside the school through this entrance, the pupils are feeling protected, imagination is smoothly taking place.

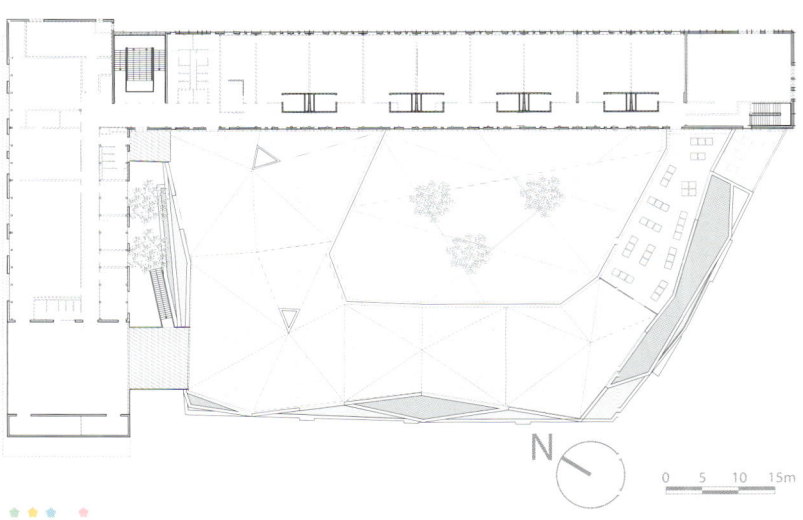

Architects : archi5 & Tecnova architecture
Country : France
Dimensions : 4338m²
Photography : Sergio Grazia
Client : City of Bezons
Project Location : Edouard Vaillant street, ZAC Coeur de Ville, Bezons

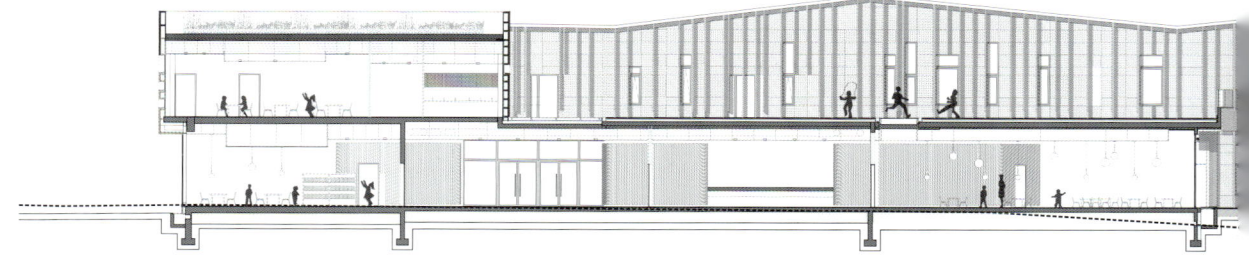

Angela Davis school Bezons

Architects : archi5 & Tecnova architecture
Country : France

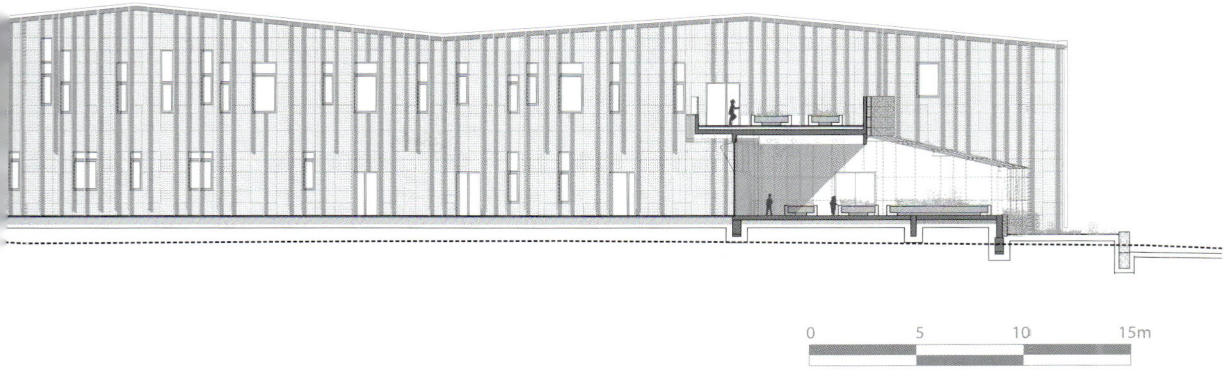

0 5 10 15m

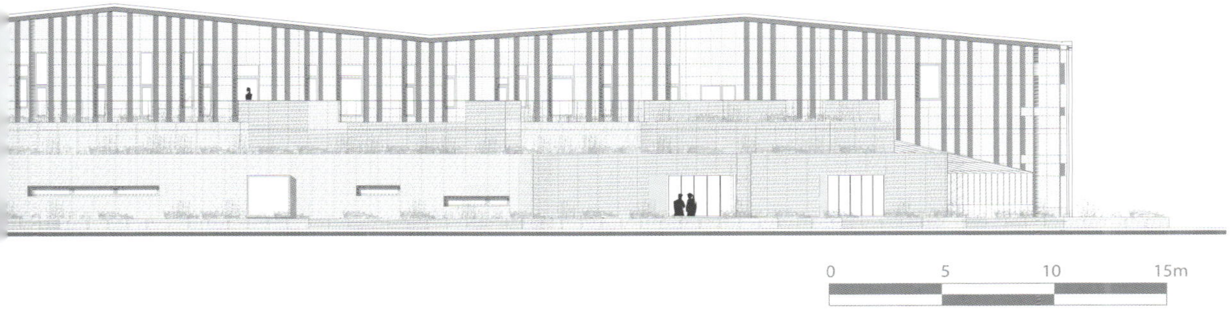

0 5 10 15m

349

350

Angela Davis school Bezons

Architects : archi5 & Tecnova architecture
Country : France

Angela Davis school Bezons

Architects : archi5 & Tecnova architecture
Country : France

Angela Davis school Bezons

Architects : archi5 & Tecnova architecture
Country : France

Jules Verne School Châtenay Malabry

The goal of this project was the profound modification of the schoo's image. We proposed an organization based on users comfort. The children are considered as the project center by giving them a qualitative learning place. From a urban scale, la Place de l'Enfance is refurbished and become a new public space and a landmark for the neighbourhood.

The urban facade unifies all parts of the school in a coherent project. Each part (infant school, primary schoo, leisure center...) remains independant but reunited in a whole renewed identity. The vegetated roof in wooden structure on the first floor connects and unifies the three emergences of existing and refurbished parts. Each volume has its function: infant school on East, primary school on West, leisure centers and common parts on central zone.

The roof and light facades, all in wooden structure allowed to lead works with less nuisances in different in an occupied site. The parts were prefabricated in workshop to be pieced together quickly and following a dry implementation. The building facades present high thermic efficiency, acoustic insulation and airtightness which is mandatory for a low consumption project. Our proposition, with its smooth and flexible geometry allows future evolutions of use while preserving the original concept. It is an additional guarantee of the sustainability of the project.

Architects : archi5
Country : France
Dimensions : 10063m²
Photography : Sergio Grazia
Client : City of Châtenay Malabry
Project Location : Jules Verne street, Châtenay Malabry

358

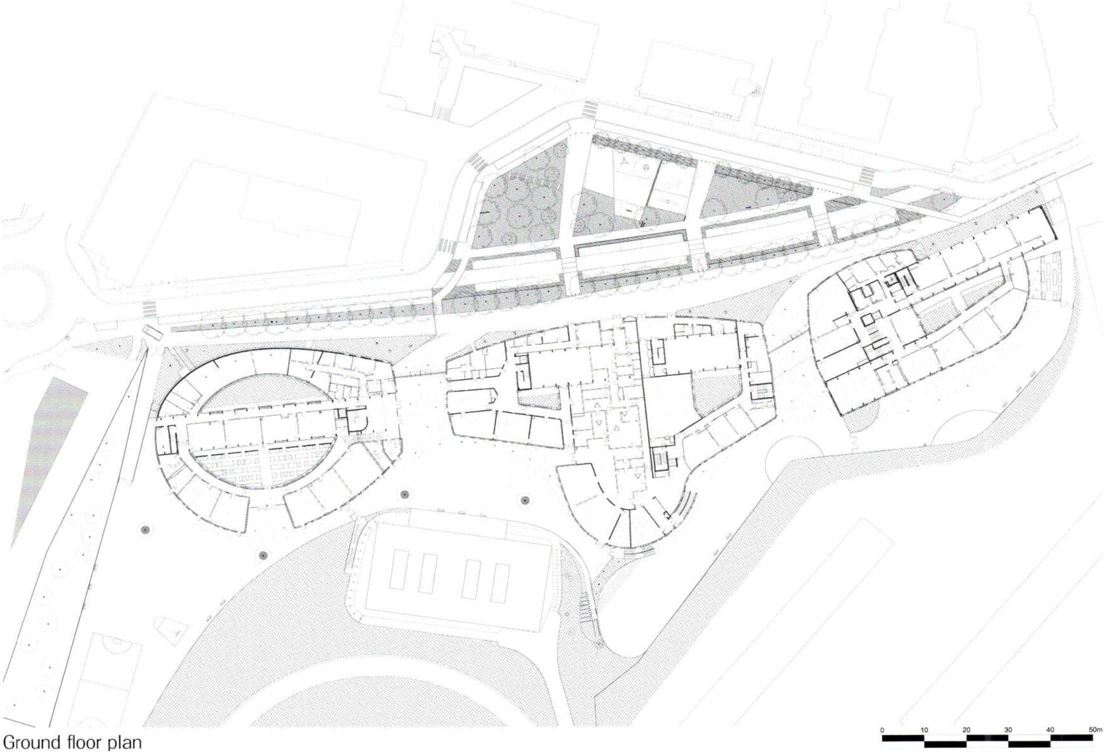

Ground floor plan

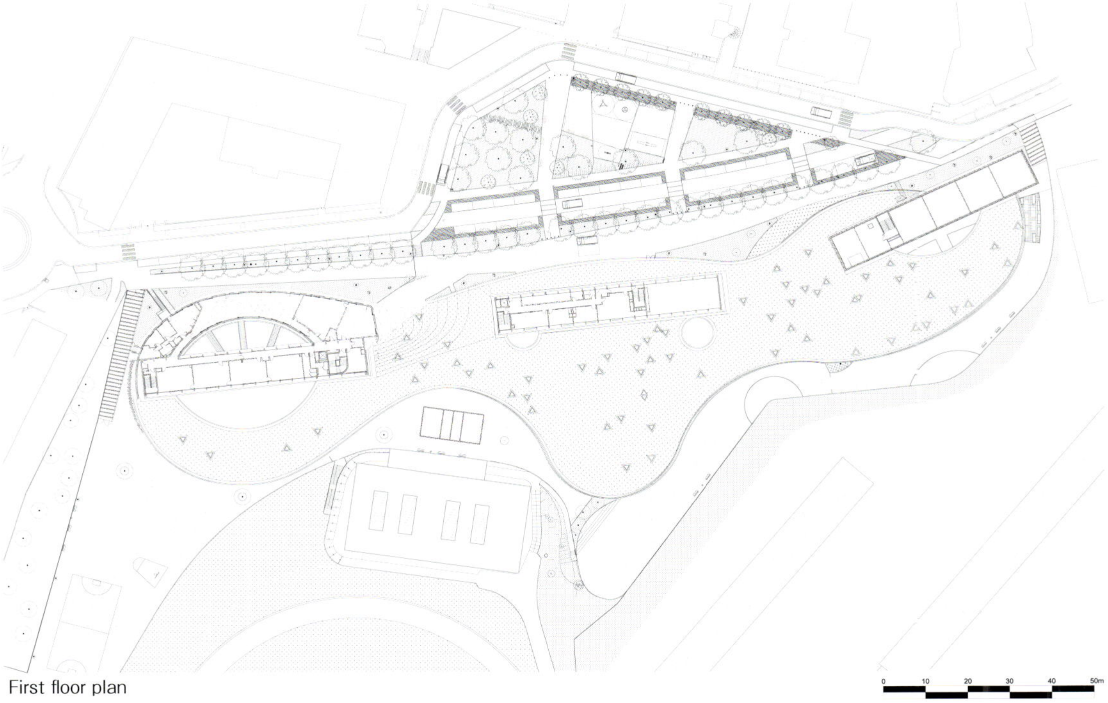

First floor plan

Jules Verne School Châtenay Malabry

Architects : archi5
Country : France

Jules Verne School Châtenay Malabry

Architects : archi5
Country : France

361

Jules Verne School Châtenay Malabry

Architects : archi5
Country : France

Jules Verne School Châtenay Malabry

Architects : archi5
Country : France

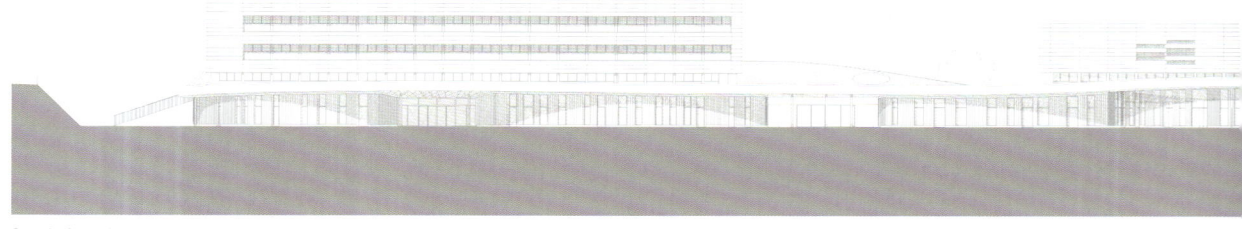

South facade

North facade

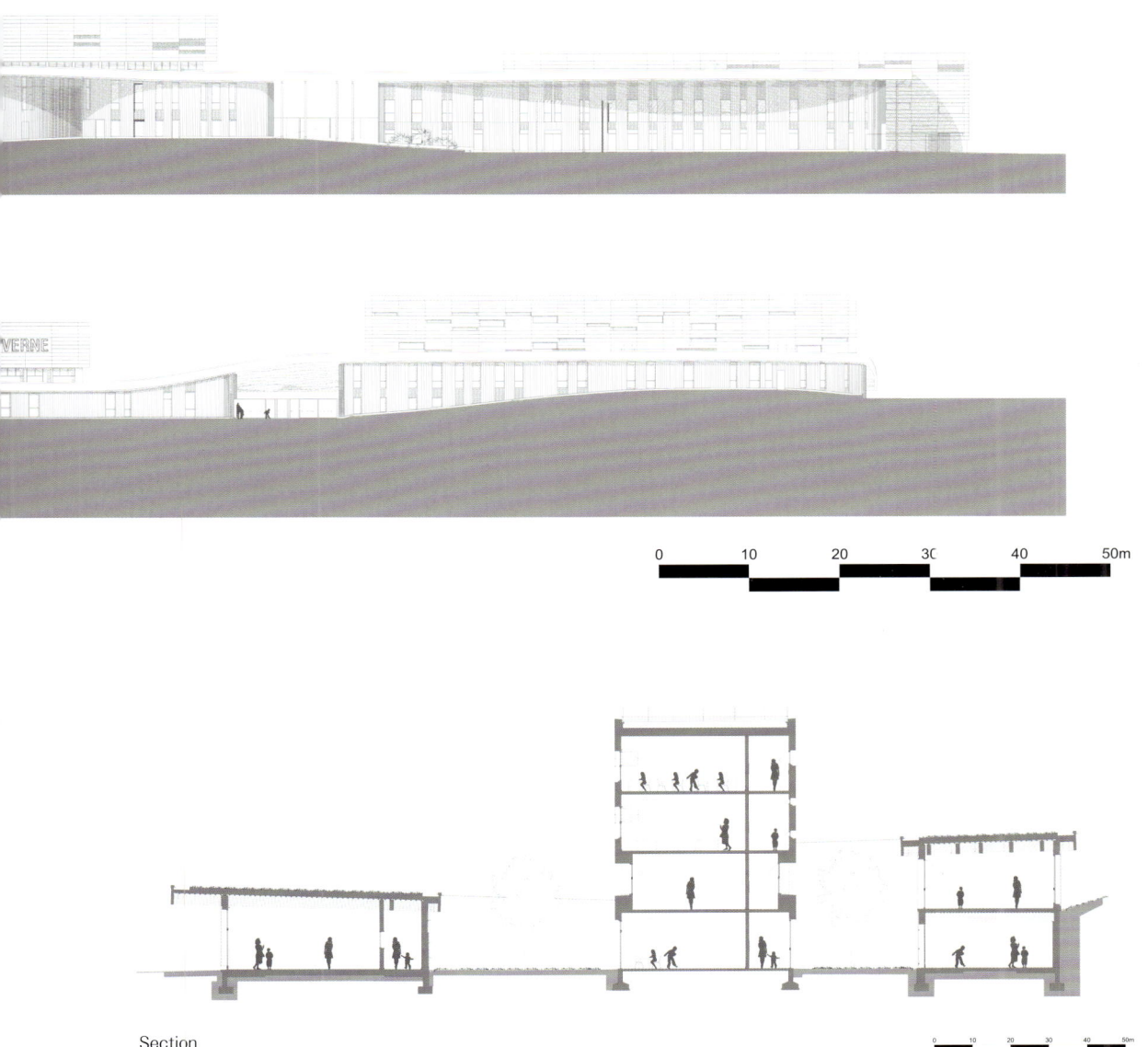

Section

Jules Verne School Châtenay Malabry

Architects : archi5
Country : France

Louise Michel high school Gisors

The purpose here is to give a high school consistent with the city of Gisors. An institution rooted in a city of human scale and rich historical references. A city which kept his medieval past and his contemporary rural environment. Historically the two high schools are adjacent, now closely linked by the administration and running, it is time to unite.

The previous running was complex. The multiplicity of access and the lack of links between the buildings were dividing the high schools.

We choosed a clear design allowing an easy orientation for the users and facilitating exchange between the two high schools. The new united high school is on both sides of the Old Eragny street. A large plaza allows arriving and access for the 1500 students and professors in total safety.

The bridge building gives access to the Louise Michel high school playground from the Louis Aragon main playground. It creates a link contributing to the unity of the whole site.

By his situation and his unifying function, the bridge building becomes the sign, the emblem of the new high school. It is also his focal point. It houses the spaces dedicated to students (school life, home, study rooms...), they are directly related to the two playgrounds. Professor's spaces are located close to the administrative parts of the two high schools.

The Louis Aragon high school hall is designed as the new central point of the new high schools. It is in the same time place for meetings and the nerve center of circulation of the entire site. It distributes access to all points of high schools: bridge building, classroom, playground, library, multipurpose room and students housings.

Architects : archi5
Country : France
Dimensions : 19150m² rehabilitated, 6400m² new
Photography : Sergio Grazia
Client : Région Normandie
Project Location : Rue Eragny, Gisors

370

Louise Michel high school Gisors

Architects : archi5
Country : France

Louise Michel high school Gisors

Architects : archi5
Country : France

Louise Michel high school Gisors

Architects : archi5
Country : France

Louise Michel high school Gisors

Architects : archi5
Country : France

378

Louise Michel high school Gisors

Architects : archi5
Country : France

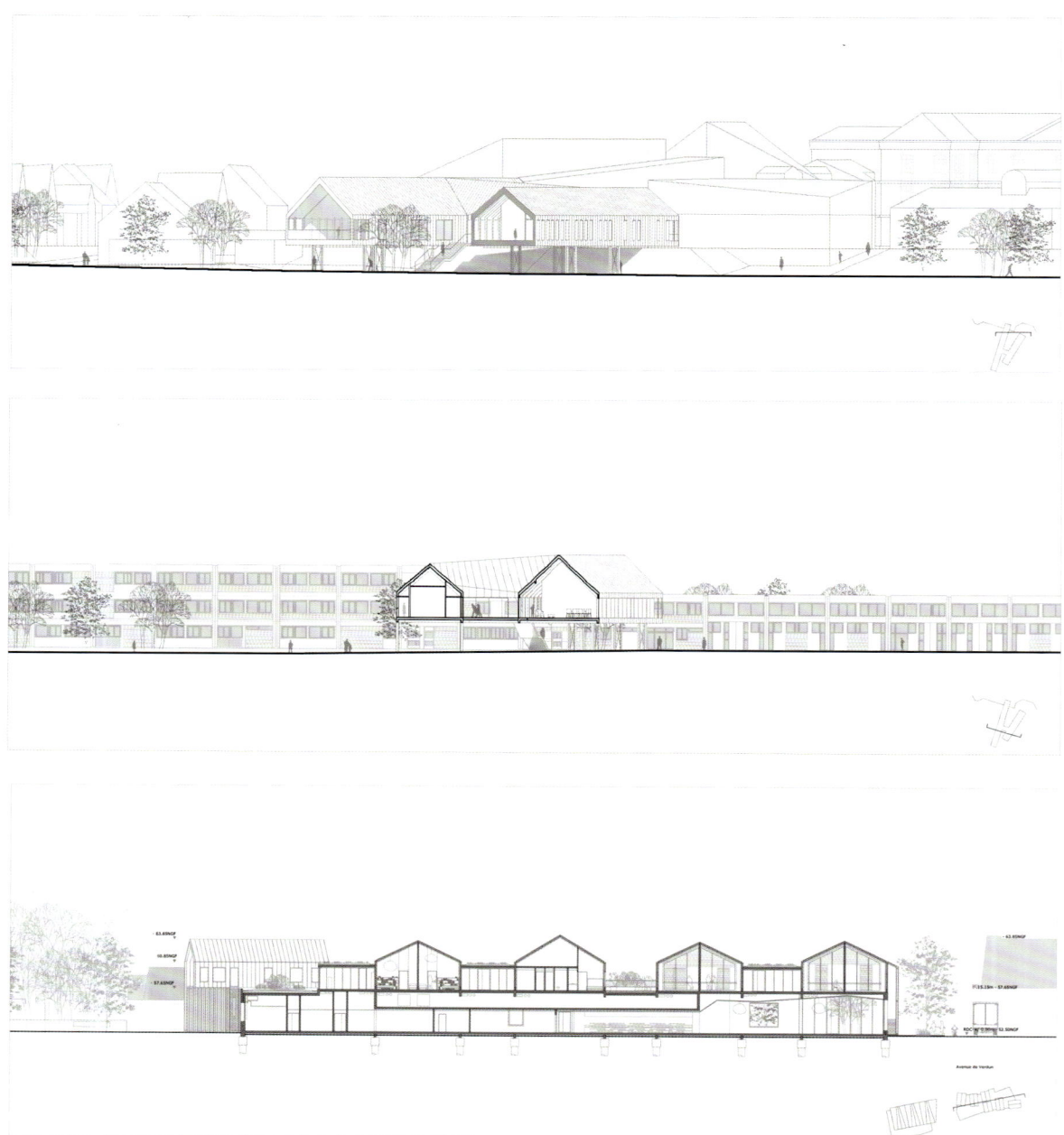

Louise Michel high school Gisors

Architects : archi5
Country : France

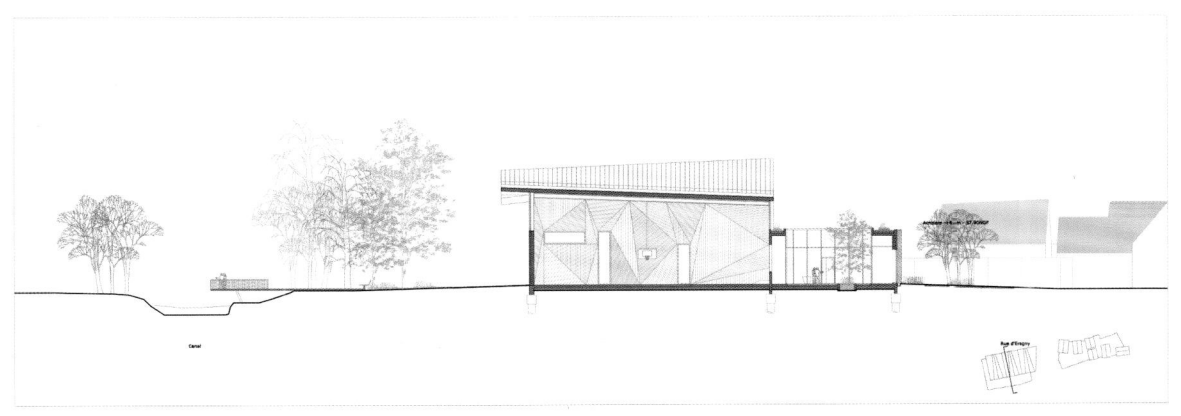
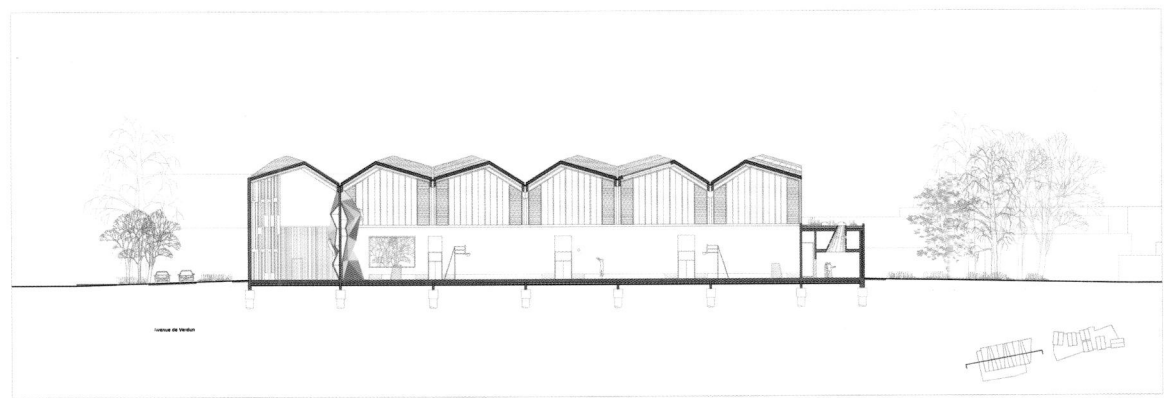
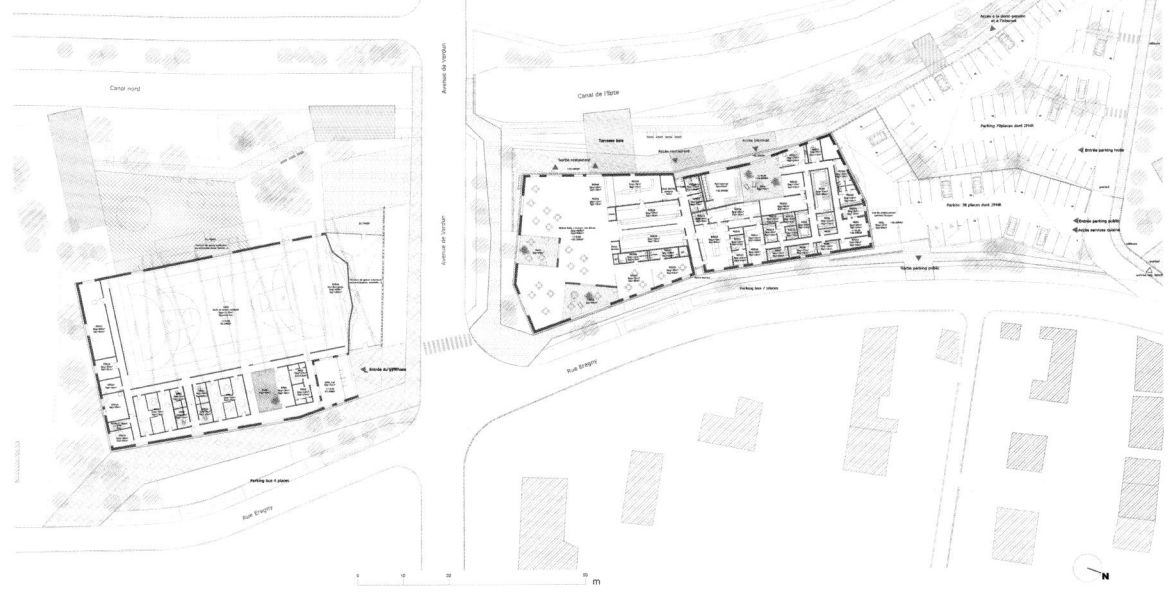

Biography

Avenier Cornejo architectes — France / 4

Christelle Avenier and Miguel Cornejo (born in Chile) founded their firm in Paris in 2008, after finishing their studies at the École supérieure de Paris Malaquais. They were selected as one of the "Europe 40 under 40" 2014 architecture firms, which awards emerging young architects. They were also nominated for the 2015 Mies van der Rohe Award and the French award "Équerred' argent" 2014 for the project "Les Lilas".

N-Martin architectural studio — Serbia / 16

Architectural studio N-Martin was founded in 2005 as a natural sequence of events and long-term work of the architect Nikola Martinovic. Our work is multidisciplinary, which means it includes architecture, furniture design, interior furnishing, urban projects, urban planning and architectural analysis and research in the fields of art and design.

Pierre-Alain Dupraz — Switzerland / 30

Pierre-Alain Dupraz Architecte ETS FAS is an architecture office based in Geneva - Switzerland, founded by Pierre-Alain Dupraz in 2002. Composed of about ten collaborators/professionals, the team mainly develops public and private projects both in Switzerland and in France.

Rh+ architecture — France / 46

The agency was created in 2000 by Alix Héaume and Adrien Robain, both DPLG architects and associate managers. In parallel with the agency's activities, the two partners are involved in several associations and institutions dedicated to the promotion of architecture: Adrien Robain was Vice-President of the Maison de l'Architecture in Ile-de-France for 8 years; Alix Héaume and Adrien Robain were part of the association "French Touch" which published, among other things, « les annuels optimisted' architecture ».

Rueda Pizarro Architects — Spain / 58

María José Pizarro and Oscar Rueda are Doctors of Architecture by the School of Architecture of Madrid -ETSAM- of the Universidad Politécnica de Madrid and by the European University of Madrid -UEM-. They teach currently at the School of Architecture of Madrid -ETSAM- and at the European University of Madrid -UEM-. In 1996 they founded their own professional office, Rueda Pizarro Architects SLP, in Madrid.

HyoMan Kim — Korea / 68

HyoMan Kim is principle of IROJE KHM Architects. He has received international awards including Iconic Awards, German Design Awards, World Architecture Community Awards, Architizer A+ Awards, ARCASIA AWARD and many kinds of domestic architecture awards.

Archivision Hirotani Studio — Japan / 78

YOSHIHIRO HIROTANI, 1956 Born in Wakayama Prefecture, Japan. 1980 Graduated from Tokyo University of Science Joined Archivision Architect & Associates. 2006 Established Archivision Hirotani Studio with YUSAKU ISHIDA. YUSAKU ISHIDA, 1969 Born in Saitama Prefecture, Japan. 1994 Graduated from Tokyo City University with Master's Degree in Architecture. 1996 Joined Archivision Architect & Associates. 2006 Established Archivision Hirotani Studio with YOSHIHIRO HIROTANI.

Kentaro Yamazaki — Japan / 92

1976 Born in Chiba. 2002 Graduated the university of Kogakuin with M.A. 2002 Worked at Irie Miyake Architects & engineers. 2008 Established Architectural design firm Yamazaki Kentaro Design Workshop. 2014 Lecture at Kogakuin University. 2017 Lecture at Tokyo University of Science. 2017 Lecture at Meiji University.

Gianni Cito — Netherlands / 102

The architect is Gianni Cito. Moke Architecten is a young and rapidly growing firm for architecture and urbanism in Amsterdam. With this growing group of 15 architects/urbanist/interior architects Moke is involved in school designs, large inner city housing schemes, the renovation and extension of a museum, two shopping centers and multiple urban plans.

HIBINOSEKKEI + Youji no Shiro — Japan / 116

Youji no Shiro, which means 'The Castle for Children' in Japanese, is the name of a section of Hibino Sekkei Architecutre, based in Kanagawa, Japan. The company was founded in 1972 and had launched the section that specialises in the design of spaces for children in 1991, reflecting the rapidly altering social situation. With fewer children continuing to develop, we became to think that existing preschool architecture where classrooms of same sizes and shapes were lined up weren't just right.

Tezuka Architects — Japan / 182

Tezuka Architects is a Japanese Architect firm based in Tokyo, Japan. Lead by the principals Takaharu and Yui Tezuka, they have provided master planning and programming, architecture and interior design as well as construction supervision since 1994, the year of their foundation.

CEBRA — Denmark / 190

CEBRA is a Danish architectural office founded in 2001 by the architects Mikkel Frost, Carsten Primdahl and Kolja Nielsen. In April 2017, architect MAA Mikkel Hallundbæk Schlesinger entered the group of partners. Based in Aarhus in Denmark and in Abu Dhabi in the UAE, CEBRA employs a multidisciplinary international staff of 50, who all share a strong passion for architecture.

ARCHITECTURE + DESIGN FOR KIDS

BUILD A DREAM

Abalosllopis architects + F-VA studio
Spain / 200

Abalosllopis architects have more than ten years of experience working across a breadth of scales and building types, from the apartment refurbishment to landscape, both in Spain and abroad.
F-VA studio, established on 2000 by the architects Enrique Fernández-Vivancos and Isabel Vernia, works on these two basic premises, taking both on to account, the different scales on which inhabit develops and human centrality as a inalienable starting point for their proposals.

Arhitektura Jure Kotnik
Slovenia / 212

Jure Kotnik, PhD., is educational architecture specialist and author of several kindergartens, schools and children's playground projects; author of several books and articles on educational architecture and design. He also works as a consultant for various international clients such as The World Bank, Council of Europe Development Bank, Steve Jobs School and others.

feld72 Architekten ZT GmbH
Austria / 256

The work of feld72 pivots on the interface of architecture, applied urbanism and art. feld72 has implemented numerous projects of various dimensions in the national and international context, a huge range including master plans, buildings, studies on urban development, interior and exhibition design, urban strategies and large-scale interventions in the urban environment.

CCDSTUDIO
Italy / 270

The CCD STUDIO WORKGROUP, through their professional research activities, focus on various spatial languages through which they aspire to create and realize contemporary architectural spaces. The three individuals that organize and coordinate the network of collaborators and consultants, was established as a working group project in 2004, following their studies in Building and Architectural Engineering at the University of Aquila.

Klab Architecture
Greece / 298

KLAB architecture (kinetic lab of architecture), was founded in 2001 by Konstantinos Labrinopoulos. It is a group of highly qualified and motivated architects who seek opportunities to create unique and intriguing urban events. Freedom of inspiration, originality in design and strict project implementation are the principles that drive the firm's continuous development earning it a considerable number of highly successful projects in Greece, U.K and South East Europe as well as various distinctions and awards throughout the years.

Mario Cucinella Architects
Italy / 306

Italian architect Mario Cucinella is amongst the most important architects practicing in Europe today with multiple award-winning international design projects. Not only is Cucinella's work lauded for design excellence but he is an undisputed global leader in sustainable practices ranging from individual residences to urban master plans. For the 2018 Venice Biennale, Mario Cucinella will be the curator of the Italian Pavilion.

ATELIER 8000
Czech Republic / 320

Martin Krupauer and Jiří Stritecký established ATELIER 8000 in 1989 driven by a desire to build with maximum creative and work freedom. They were at the same time aware of responsibility for the whole process from the design to the end of construction. The architectural studio has its seat in České Budějovice with a branch in Prague; 55 people work together in these two offices: architects, building engineers and other staff necessary for a professional operation of an architectural office.

KÜHNLEIN Architektur
Germany / 330

The architects try to develop and improve the habitats internally and externally. Holistic approaches and interdisciplinary approach are important to them. The focus is on the human being as a benchmark, nature as a valuable resource. Responsible handling of the inventory is essential to our work. With simple, clear ideas and concepts, they want to plan and build ecologically and sustainably.

Vincent Parreira
France / 338

Vincent Parreira is a French-Portuguese architect born in Paris in 1969. He graduated with a degree in architecture from École Nationale Supérieured' Architecture de Paris La Villette and founded his studio AAVP ARCHITECTURE in Paris in 2000. His ambition is to create projects that are brimming with sentiment.

archi5 Studio
France / 346

archi5 was founded in 2003, the fruit of its founders' common agency experience and the approach they share to architecture. The agency uses its acumen and know-how to instill this ethos throughout and to guarantee its continuity. Establishing strategic links with the best technical partners and expert consultants the agency further develops its skills. The success archi5 has achieved in public contract tenders and the private sector has allowed the agency to expand its horizons beyond Europe.

ACKNOWLEDGEMENTS

DESIGNERBOOKS (DB) sincerely thanks all the artists, designers and companies that contributed to this book, meanwhile thank all the staff, translators and printing companies involved in the design and production of this book. Without their efforts and contributions, the book will not be presented to readers in a graceful manner. We will pay attention to all the valuable suggestions from all our friends, and DB will make every effort to do well in every book.

JOIN US

If you want to join DESIGNERBOOKS for future projects and publications, please submit your work and information to
edit@designerbooks.com.cn